Drawing

A STUDIO GUIDE

Drawing

A STUDIO GUIDE

BY LU BRO

W · W · NORTON & COMPANY

New York · London

W. W. Norton & Company, Inc. 500 Fifth Avenue, New York, N.Y. 10110
W. W. Norton & Company Ltd. 37 Great Russell Street, London WC1B 3NU

Published simultaneously in Canada by
Penguin Books Canada Ltd,
2801 John Street, Markham, Ontario L3R 1B4.

Book design by Antonina Krass

Library of Congress Cataloging in Publication Data
Bro, Lu.
Drawing, a studio guide.
Bibliography: p.
Includes index.
1. Drawing—Technique. I. Title.
NC735.B69 1978 741.2 78-12136

ISBN 0-393-01199-2
ISBN 0-393-95018-2 PBK
3 4 5 6 7 8 9 0

FOR MY CHILDREN

Sarah Luanne and Gustav Andrew

CONTENTS

LIST OF ILLUSTRATIONS   xi

PREFACE   xxiii

ACKNOWLEDGMENTS   xxvii

Part One | INTRODUCTION

1 · STARTING: PROCESS AND MEDIA   3

Part Two | THE CONTOUR LINE

2 · BLIND CONTOUR AND BALANCE IN COMPOSITION   27

3 · NEGATIVE CONTOUR   44

4 · ANIMAL STUDIES IN CONTOUR   49

5 · IMAGE INVERSION   57

6 · CROSS CONTOUR   59

7 · DISTORTIONS   65

8 · LINEAR PERSPECTIVE   70

9 · FORESHORTENING IN CONTOUR   106

[*vii*]

Part Three | THE GESTURE

10 · GENERAL GESTURE 127

11 · ACTION GESTURE 132

12 · BODY STRESS IN GESTURE 137

13 · REVERSE GESTURE 141

14 · GESTURES OF WALKS AND GESTURAL COMPOSITION 143

Part Four | TRANSITION INTO VALUES:
VOLUME AND PATTERN

15 · A PROBLEM IN SCULPTURE—HEADS 153

16 · VALUES IN GESTURE/THE ELONGATED GESTURE 160

17 · THREE-TONE PATTERN IN CONTOUR 165

Part Five | VALUE

18 · VALUE STUDIES 185

19 · REVERSE VALUE STUDIES 192

20 · VALUE IN DRAPERY 196

21 · SAME SUBJECT—THREE LIGHTING POSITIONS 206

22 · CROSSHATCH 209

23 · TWO-DAY STUDY OF LANDSCAPE STRUCTURE 215

Part Six | ANALYTICAL TRACINGS,
CRITICISM, AND EXPRESSION

24 · ANALYTICAL TRACINGS: MORE ON COMPOSITION 225

25 · RESPONSIVE ANALYSIS: A CRITICAL METHOD 232

26 · EXPRESSION 246

Contents

Part Seven | SOME EXPERIMENTATION

27 · REPETITION OF IMAGES   255

28 · SELECTED COMPOSING   260

29 · COLLAGE AND MIXED MEDIA   263

30 · VARIATIONS   270

Part Eight | MATTING

31 · MATTING: SIMPLE AND STANDARD   293

NOTES   309

BIBLIOGRAPHY   311

INDEX   315

STUDENT CREDITS   320

PHOTO CREDITS   321

LIST OF ILLUSTRATIONS

FRONTISPIECE

Leonardo da Vinci: *Study of Hands,* from *The Notebooks of Leonardo* (ca. 1489). Silverpoint heightened with white on pink prepared paper, 8⁷⁄₁₆″ × 5¹⁵⁄₁₆″. Royal Library, Windsor Castle, London.   ii

PREFACE ILLUSTRATION

Wayne Thiebaud: *Toys* (1971). Charcoal on paper, 20″ × 26″. Collection, the artist.   xxv

FIGURES

1.1.	Bone drawing as a virtual copy.	5
1.2.	Bone drawing with composition in mind.	5
1.3.	Kinds of paper.	8
1.4.	Kinds of pencils.	9
1.5.	Charcoal, chalk, crayons.	10
1.6.	Erasers.	11
1.7.	Ink and brushes.	12
1.8.	Pens.	14
1.9.	Mat boards.	15
1.10.	Assorted supplies.	15
2.1.	Hans Holbein the Younger: *The Family of Sir Thomas More* (1526). Pen and ink, 15⁷⁄₁₆″ × 20¼″. Offentliche Kunstsammlung, Basel.	19
2.2.	Philipp Otto Runge: *Lily with Hovering Genii* (1809). Pen and ink, 26½″ × 17¹¹⁄₁₆″. Kunsthalle, Hamburg.	20

2.3. Henri Matisse: *Reclining Nude* (1937). Charcoal, 15″ × 19″. Art Institute of Chicago.　　　21

2.4. Pablo Picasso: study for the painting *Pipes of Pan* (ca. 1923). Charcoal, 25³⁄₁₆″ × 19⁵⁄₁₆″. Art Institute of Chicago.　　　22

2.5. Jean-Auguste-Dominique Ingres: *Charles-François Mallet, Civil Engineer* (1809). Pencil, 10⁹⁄₁₆″ × 8⅜″. Art Institute of Chicago.　　　23

2.6. Hans Holbein the Younger: *Portrait of Frau Burgermeister Dorothea Meyer* (ca. 1535). Colored chalk, 15⅜″ × 11″. Museum Faesch, Basel.　　　24

2.7. Katsushika Hokusai: *Self-Portrait* (ca. 1845). Brush and ink. Musée Guimet, Paris.　　　25

2.8. John L. Weinkein: *Great-Grandfather* (1977). Colored pencil, 20″ × 24″. Private collection.　　　26

2.9. *Stags (or Reindeer) Crossing a Stream with Fish* (prehistoric). Impression rolled from an engraved staff, a reindeer antler, 9¾″ long, Lortet (Hautes-Pyrénées), France. Musée des Antiquités Nationales, Saint-Germain-en-Laye.　　　28

2.10. The Achilles Painter: white-ground lekythos (ca. 440 B.C.). Pottery, 15″ high. British Museum, London.　　　28

2.11. Pablo Picasso: *La Source* (1921). Pencil, 19″ × 25¼″. Museum of Modern Art, New York.　　　29

2.12. Student drawing, wrist to finger, in blind contour. Pencil on newsprint.　　　30

2.13. Student drawing, wrist to finger, in blind contour. Pencil on newsprint.　　　30

2.14. Student drawing of a hand in blind contour. Pencil on newsprint.　　　31

2.15. Student drawing of a hand in blind contour. Pencil on newsprint.　　　31

2.16. Student drawing of a shoe in blind contour. Pencil on newsprint.　　　32

2.17. Student drawing of a shoe in blind contour. Pencil on newsprint.　　　33

2.18. Student drawing of a profile in blind contour. Pencil on white drawing paper.　　　34

2.19. Student drawing of a profile in blind contour. Pencil on white drawing paper.　　　34

2.20. Student drawing of a model in a chair in blind contour. Pencil on newsprint.　　　35

2.21. Student drawing of a felt contour. Pencil on newsprint.　　　35

2.22. Student drawing of a felt contour. Pencil on newsprint.　　　35

2.23. Albrecht Altdorfer: *Battle of Alexander* (1529). Lime panel, 62¼″ × 47¼″. Alte Pinakothek, Munich.　　　37

2.24. Johannes Bosboom: church interior (ca. 1860). Water color and gouache over pencil, 16⅛″ × 12¼″. Art Institute of Chicago.　　　38

2.25. Joseph Mallord William Turner: *The Slave Ship* (1840). Oil painting, 35¾″ × 48″. Museum of Fine Arts, Boston.　　　38

2.26. Heinrich Voegler: *Eine Liebe ("A Love")* (1896). Etching, 13¾″ × 14⅞″. Des Moines Art Center.　　　39

List of Illustrations

2.27. John Singer Sargent: *The Pailleron Children* (1881). Oil painting, 60″ × 69″. Des Moines Art Center.   40

2.28. Raffaello Sanzio, known as Raphael: *Baldassare Castiglione* (1516). Oil painting, 32¼″ × 26⅜″. Louvre, Paris.   40

2.29. Li Ch'eng (Ying-ch'iu): *Buddhist Temple amid Clearing Mountain Peaks*. Ink and slight color on silk, 44″ × 22″. Nelson Gallery–Atkins Museum of Fine Arts, Kansas City.   41

2.30. George Caleb Bingham: *Fur Traders Descending the Missouri* (ca. 1845). Oil painting, 29″ × 36½″. Metropolitan Museum of Art, New York.   42

2.31. Peter Paul Rubens: *The Small Final Judgment* (ca. 1620). Oil painting, 72³⁄₁₆″ × 46⅞″. Alte Pinakothek, Munich.   42

3.1. Still life showing positive shapes.   45

3.2. Still life showing negative shapes.   45

3.3. Negative shapes.   47

3.4. Negative shapes regardless of depth.   47

3.5. Horizontal composition on a vertical sheet.   47

3.6. Vertical composition on a horizontal sheet.   48

4.1. Housebook Master: *Dog Scratching Itself* (ca. 1480–1490). Engraving. Rijksmuseum, Amsterdam.   50

4.2. Composition too low on the page.   51

4.3. Composition layout with ½-inch lines.   52

4.4. Student contour drawing of a mounted animal. Pencil on white drawing paper.   52

4.5. Animal form suggested with contour (tail).   52

4.6. Student contour drawing of a mounted animal. Pencil on white drawing paper.   54

4.7. Student contour drawing of a mounted duck. Pencil on white drawing paper.   54

4.8. Gnosis: *Stag Hunt* (ca. 300 B.C.). Floor mosaic. Pella Museum.   56

5.1. Inverted image.   58

6.1. Engraved lines of a stamp showing cross-contour lines.   60

6.2. Student drawing of a still life in cross contour. Pencil on newsprint.   61

6.3. Student drawing of drapery in cross contour. Pencil on white drawing paper.   62

6.4. Student drawing of a still life in cross contour. Pencil on white drawing paper.   62

6.5. German: page from Virgil's *Aeneid* (1502). Woodcut, 12⅛″ × 8⅜″. Des Moines Art Center.   63

6.6. Vincent Willem Van Gogh: *Grove of Cypresses* (1889). Reed pen with ink over pencil, 24¹¹⁄₁₆″ × 18⁵⁄₁₆″. Art Institute of Chicago.   63

7.1. Francesco Maria Mazzuoli, known as Parmigianino: *Self-Portrait* (1524). Panel, diameter 9⅝″. Kunsthistorisches Museum, Vienna.   66

7.2. Student contour drawing of a distorted image. Pencil on newsprint. 67

7.3. Student contour drawing of a distorted image. Pencil on newsprint. 67

7.4. Student contour drawing of a distorted image. Pencil on white drawing paper. 68

7.5. Hans Holbein the Younger: *Jean de Dinteville and Georges de Selves, or The Ambassadors* (1533). Oil and tempera on panel, 6′ 9½″ × 6′ 10½″. National Gallery, London. 69

8.1. *Last Judgment* (early eleventh century). Ottonian miniature from the *Book of Pericopes* of Henry II. Bayerische Staatsbibliothek, Munich. 71

8.2. The Foundry Painter: *Lapith and Centaur* (ca. 490–480 B.C.). Interior of an Attic red-figured kylix. Staatliche Antikensammlungen, Munich. 72

8.3. Inlay on a soundbox from a harp (ca. 2685 B.C.). From Ur, wood with inlaid gold, lapis lazuli, and shell. University Museum, Philadelphia. 72

8.4. Albrecht Dürer: illustration from *Underweisung der Messung mit dem Birkel und Richtscheit* (1525). Woodcut. 74

8.5. The eye, the inverted image on the retina, the light rays or sight lines, and the cone of vision. 74

8.6. Sight lines or light rays intersecting the picture plane become the image of the object seen in perspective. 74

8.7. Albrecht Dürer: *Draftsman Drawing a Lute* (1525). Woodcut, 5³⁄₁₆″ × 7³⁄₁₆″. 75

8.8. Albrecht Dürer: *Draftsman Drawing a Portrait* (1525). Woodcut, 5³⁄₁₆″ × 5⅞″. 76

8.9. Simone Martini: *Annunciation* (1333). Panel, 104⅛″ × 120⅛″. Uffizi Gallery, Florence. 76

8.10. *Byzantine Christ* (ca. thirteenth century). Detail of the Deësis mosaic, Hagia Sophia, Istanbul. 77

8.11. Tommaso Guidi, known as Masaccio: *Trinity* (1425). Fresco, 21′ 10½″ × 10′ 5″. Santa Maria Novella, Florence. 78

8.12. Diminution, foreshortening, convergence. 80

8.13a. Horizon line, high. 81

8.13b. Horizon line, middle. 81

8.13c. Horizon line, low. 81

8.13d. Andrea Mantegna: *St. James Led to His Execution* (ca. 1455). Pen drawing, 6⅛″ × 9¼″. British Museum, London. 81

8.13e. Winslow Homer: *The Morning Bell* (ca. 1866). Oil on canvas, 24″ × 38¼″. Yale University Art Gallery, New Haven. 81

8.13f. Albrecht Altdorfer: *Battle of Alexander* (1529). Lime panel, 62¼″ × 47¼″. Alte Pinakothek, Munich. 81

8.13g. Hilaire Germain Edgar Degas: *Estelle Musson* (ca. 1872). Pastel, 25″ × 22⅞″. Metropolitan Museum of Art, New York. 81

8.13h. Maurice-Quentin de La Tour: *Portrait of Jean-Marc Nattier* (ca. 1760). Pastel, 13¼″ × 10⅞″. Musée de Picardie, Amiens. 81

List of Illustrations

8.13i. Hilaire Germain Edgar Degas: *Portrait of Mademoiselle Lisle* (ca. 1869). Pastel and red crayon on buff paper, 8⅝″ × 10⅛″. Metropolitan Museum of Art, New York. 81

8.14. The cone of vision within which the picture plane is placed on which the perspective image is viewed. 82

8.15. Families of receding parallel lines converge to separate vanishing points, each of which is beyond the boundary of the picture plane. 84

8.16. "Those things seen within a larger angle appear larger and those things seen within a smaller angle appear smaller." 85

8.17. Placing the vertical vanishing point can be done by pointing in the same direction the parallel vertical lines recede. 86

8.18. The cube at eye level with one corner aligned with your central sight line. 88

8.19. By turning the cube to the right, the left vanishing point moves farther from the corner than the right vanishing point. The central sight line does not remain aligned with the corner. 88

8.20. Now the former right vanishing point and the left vanishing point are an infinite distance apart, and a new single vanishing point is established. 88

8.21. A three-point perspective cube has no side parallel to the picture plane, and three groups of parallels converge to three separate vanishing points. 89

8.22. Using a sheet of tracing paper, trace the receding parallel lines to the vanishing point on this one-point perspective of a house interior. 91

8.23. Using a sheet of tracing paper, trace the receding parallel lines to their vanishing points on this two-point perspective of Timberlake Playhouse. 91

8.24. Using a sheet of tracing paper, trace the receding parallel lines to their vanishing points on this three-point perspective of the Shimer belltower. 91

8.25. A building drawn in contour line. 93

8.26. The diagonals of any square or rectangle will always intersect at the exact center, whether the square or rectangle is true or in perspective. 93

8.27. The center of a circle encased by a square is found at the intersection of the diagonals of the square, whether true or in perspective. 95

8.28. The ellipse (circle in perspective), encased in a rectangle and divided into four equal sections, forms axis lines. 95

8.29. The pivotal line for a circle in perspective is the minor axis of the ellipse. 95

8.30. The minor axis becomes the center line of the lamp stand and the bar of the barbells. 96

8.31. Francesco di Gentile da Fabriano: *Nativity*, from *Adoration of the Magi* predella (1421). Panel, 12¼″ × 29½″. Uffizi Gallery, Florence. 97

8.32. Pablo Picasso: *Ambroise Vollard* (1909–1910). Oil on canvas, 36″ × 26½″. Pushkin Museum, Moscow. 97

8.33. Georges de La Tour: *St. Joseph the Carpenter* (ca. 1645). Oil on canvas, 38½″ × 25″. Louvre, Paris.   98

8.34. Winslow Homer: *The Morning Bell* (ca. 1866). Oil on canvas, 24″ × 38¼″. Yale University Art Gallery, New Haven.   99

8.35. The length of a cast shadow depends on the angle of the light rays.   100

8.36. Vertical lines will cast shadows in the direction of the light rays, on a plane. In this case a candle was used, and the shadows radiate from the light source.   100

8.37. Again, vertical lines will cast shadows in the direction of the light rays, on a plane. In this case a light bulb was used, and the shadows radiate from the light source.   101

8.38. When the sun's rays are not parallel to the picture plane, there will be three sets of convergence points.   101

8.39. A line parallel to a plane casts a shadow parallel to itself.   102

8.40. Remember, vertical lines cast shadows in the direction of the light rays, on a plane, and a line parallel to a plane casts a shadow parallel to itself.   103

8.41. Pietro Berrettini, known as Pietro da Cortona: *Glorification of the Reign of Urban VIII* (1633–1639). Detail of ceiling fresco, Palazzo Barberini, Rome.   104

9.1. Andrea Mantegna: *St. James Led to His Execution* (ca. 1455). Pen drawing, 6⅛″ × 9¼″. British Museum, London.   107

9.2. Andrea Mantegna: *St. James Led to His Execution* (ca. 1455). Fresco. Ovetari Chapel, Church of the Eremitani, Padua.   107

9.3. James Montgomery Flagg: *I Want You*. World War I poster.   108

9.4. Jacopo Robusti, known as Tintoretto: *Lying Man* (ca. 1565). Chalk, 7⅟₁₆″ × 10¹³⁄₁₆″. Art Institute of Chicago.   109

9.5. Peter Paul Rubens: *Studies of Arms and Legs* (ca. 1625). Black chalk heightened with some white, 13¾″ × 9⁷⁄₁₆″. Museum Boymans–Van Beuningen, Rotterdam.   109

9.6. Piero della Francesca: *Man's Head*, from *De prospectiva pingendi* (ca. 1470).   110

9.7. Establishing lines.   112

9.8. Andrea Mantegna: *The Dead Christ* (1570). Tempera on canvas, 26¾″ × 31¾″. Brera Picture Gallery, Milan.   113

10.1. Giacomo Balla: *Dynamism of a Dog on a Leash* (1912). Oil on canvas, 35″ × 45½″. George F. Goodyear and the Buffalo Fine Arts Academy, New York.   117

10.2. Eugène Delacroix: *Mounted Arab Attacking a Panther* (ca. 1840). Graphic pencil, 9½″ × 8″. Fogg Art Museum, Harvard University, Cambridge, Massachusetts.   118

10.3. Eugène Delacroix: *The Sultan on Horseback* (ca. 1845). Pen and ink, 8⅓″ × 6″. Louvre, Paris.   119

List of Illustrations

10.4. Alberto Giacometti: *Seated Man* (1953). Pencil, 19¹³⁄₁₆″ × 12¹³⁄₁₆″. Wallraf-Richartz Museum, Cologne.   120

10.5. Joseph Mallord William Turner: *Boats Towing Men-of-War,* from the *Cyfarthfa Sketchbook* (ca. 1800). Water color, 11½″ × 18″. British Museum, London.   121

10.6. Auguste Rodin: *Standing Nude* (ca. 1900–1905). Pencil and water color, 17⅝″ × 12½″. Art Institute of Chicago.   122

10.7. Pietro Falca, known as Pietro Longhi: *Venetian Wine Shop* (ca. 1750). Pen and brownish wash, 7¾″ × 11⅛″. Art Institute of Chicago.   123

10.8. Emil Nolde: *Harbor* (ca. 1900). Brush and India ink, 12¾″ × 18⁵⁄₁₆″. Art Institute of Chicago.   124

10.9. Ann Poor: *Tying Psycho Patient to a Litter* (1945). Ink and wash, 18⅞″ × 25¹³⁄₁₆″. Art Institute of Chicago.   125

10.10. Pierre-Paul Prud'hon: sheet of studies (ca. 1808). Black ink with brush, 11⅜″ × 17⅜″. Art Institute of Chicago.   126

10.11. Skull drawn with a rapid, jerky line.   128

10.12. Lamp drawn in gesture.   128

10.13. Student drawing of a figure in gesture. Pencil on newsprint.   129

10.14. Student drawing of a figure in gesture. Pencil on newsprint.   130

10.15. Student drawing of a figure in gesture. Pencil on newsprint.   130

11.1. Leonardo da Vinci: *A Rearing Horse* (1504), study for *The Battle of Anghiari*. Red chalk, 6″ × 5⅝″. Royal Library, Windsor Castle, London.   133

11.2. Action gesture, a student drawing of a figure in motion. Pencil on newsprint.   135

11.3. Action gesture, a student drawing of a figure in motion. Pencil on newsprint.   135

11.4. Action gesture, a student drawing of a figure in motion. Pencil on newsprint.   136

12.1. Body stress drawn in gesture. Ink on newsprint.   138

12.2. Body stress drawn in gesture. Conte crayon on newsprint.   140

12.3. Body stress drawn in gesture. Graphite on newsprint.   140

14.1. A student's interpretation in gesture of a waitress walking. Conte crayon on newsprint.   145

14.2. A student's interpretation in gesture of a man running with a racket. Graphite on newsprint.   147

14.3. Gestural composition of stairs and a doorway.   147

14.4. Frank Brangwyn: *Springtime* (1919). Oil on canvas, 19¾″ × 29½″. Des Moines Art Center.   148

15.1. Jacob Epstein: *Portrait of Albert Einstein* (1933). Bronze, 16¾″ high. Des Moines Art Center.   154

15.2. Scale drawing of a head, front and side.   157

15.3. Simple armature.   158

15.4.   Head, front, a student sculpture.   158

15.5.   Head, side.   158

16.1.   Henry Moore: *Women Winding Wool* (1949). Water color and crayon,
        13¾″ × 25″. Museum of Modern Art, New York.   161

16.2.   A student drawing in continuous gesture. Ink on oaktag.   163

16.3.   A student drawing in value gesture. Graphite on newsprint.   164

16.4.   A student drawing in continuous gesture with values. Ink on white
        drawing paper.   164

17.1.   Attic: Dipylon vase (eighth century B.C.). 42½″ high. Metropolitan Mu-
        seum of Art, New York.   166

17.2.   The Arkesilas Painter: Laconian cup (ca. 565–560 B.C.). Pottery, 7¹³⁄₁₆″
        height, 14¹⁵⁄₁₆″ diameter. Bibliothèque Nationale, Paris.   167

17.3.   Douris: *Eos and Memnon* (ca. 490–480 B.C.). Interior of an Attic red-
        figured kylix, 10½″ diameter. Louvre, Paris.   167

17.4.   A student three-tone drawing using sepia and India ink on oaktag.   169

17.5.   A student three-tone drawing using orange, white, and India ink on
        oaktag.   170

17.6.   A student three-tone drawing using persimmon, white, and India ink on
        oaktag.   170

17.7.   A student three-tone drawing using red, white, and India ink on oaktag.   170

18.1.   Claude Lorrain: *The Tiber above Rome, View from Monte Mario* (ca.
        1640). Brush and bistre wash, 7⅜″ × 10⅝″. British Museum, London.   175

18.2.   Odilon Redon: *The Reader* (1892). Lithograph, 12³⁄₁₆″ × 9⁵⁄₁₆″. Sotheby
        Parke Bernet, London.   176

18.3.   Ignace Henri Joseph Théodore Fantin-Latour: *Bouquet of Roses* (1879).
        Lithograph, 16⁵⁄₁₆″ × 13⅞″. Des Moines Art Center.   177

18.4.   Charles Sheeler: *Nude Torso* (ca. 1924). Pencil, 4½″ × 6⁵⁄₁₆″. Art In-
        stitute of Chicago.   178

18.5.   Pieter Cornelis Mondriaan: *Trees by the River Gein* (ca. 1902). Char-
        coal, 18⅜″ × 24½″. Art Institute of Chicago.   179

18.6.   Francesco Guardi: *Adoration of the Shepherds* (ca. 1750). Pen and ink
        with brown and gray wash over red chalk, 15¼″ × 20⅜″. Art Institute
        of Chicago.   180

18.7.   Mary Cassatt: *Nicolle and Her Mother* (ca. 1900). Pastel, 25⅛″ × 20¾″.
        Des Moines Art Center.   181

18.8.   Jean-Baptiste Carpeaux: *Seated Woman* (ca. 1850). Black and white
        chalk, 8⅞″ × 6⅛″. Art Institute of Chicago.   182

18.9.   Georges Seurat: *The Artist's Mother Seated before a Window* (ca. 1882).
        Black crayon over traces of brown ink, 6¼″ × 4¾″. Metropolitan Mu-
        seum of Art, New York.   183

18.10. Berthe Morisot: *Self-Portrait* (1885). Pastel, 18″ × 14″. Art Institute of
        Chicago.   184

18.11. Two types of value scales.   185

List of Illustrations

18.12. M. C. Escher: *Drawing Hands* (1948). Lithograph, 11¼″ × 13⅜″. Gemeentemuseum, The Hague.   186

18.13. A bottle drawn as an isolated shape. Charcoal on white drawing paper.   189

18.14. A student drawing of a still life with value shapes left as planes. Charcoal on charcoal paper.   189

18.15. A student drawing of a still life integrating value shapes with volumes. Charcoal on white drawing paper.   190

18.16. A student drawing of a still life integrating value shapes throughout the composition. Charcoal on newsprint.   190

18.17. A student drawing of a still life inferring depth. Charcoal on charcoal paper.   190

19.1. A student drawing of a hallway using reverse value. White chalk on black charcoal paper.   194

19.2. A student drawing of a landscape using reverse value. White chalk on black charcoal paper.   194

20.1. Lorenzo di Credi: *Saint Bartholomew* (ca. 1510). Pencil, white and red chalk on brown paper, 15¹³⁄₁₆″ × 10⅝″. Louvre, Paris.   197

20.2. A student drawing of the structure of drapery over which values were stroked.   200

20.3. A student drawing of the structure of drapery over which values were stroked.   200

20.4. Andrea Mantegna: *St. James Led to His Execution* (ca. 1455). Pen drawing, 6⅛″ × 9¼″. British Museum, London.   202

20.5. The Master of Flémalle (Robert Campin?): *The Merode Altarpiece*, center panel (ca. 1425–1428). Oil on wood, 25³⁄₁₆″ × 24⅞″. The Cloisters Collection, Metropolitan Museum of Art, New York.   202

20.6. Alessandro di Mariano dei Filipepi, known as Botticelli: *The Three Graces*, detail from the *Primavera* (ca. 1478). Tempera on wood panel. Uffizi Gallery, Florence.   203

20.7. Johannes Vermeer: *Artist in His Studio* (ca. 1665–1670). Oil on canvas, 52″ × 44″. Kunsthistorisches Museum, Vienna.   203

20.8. Jean-Auguste-Dominique Ingres: *Napoleon As Emperor* (1806). Oil on canvas, 8′ 7″ × 5′ 5″. Musée de L'Armée, Paris.   204

20.9. Gustave Doré: *Scripture Reader in a Night Refuge*, from *London: A Pilgrimage* (ca. 1870). Wood engraving, 9⁵⁄₁₆″ × 7½″.   205

21.1. Light source to the left.   208

21.2. Light source to the middle.   208

21.3. Light source to the right.   208

22.1. Jacques Villon: *Renée de Trois Quarts* (1911). Drypoint, 21¼″ × 16″. Baltimore Museum of Art.   210

22.2. Giorgio Morandi: *Large Still Life with Coffee Pot* (1933). Etching, 9¹⁵⁄₁₆″ × 13¹¹⁄₁₆″. Art Institute of Chicago.   210

22.3. William Hogarth: *Simon Lord Lovat* (1746). Etching, 14¼″ × 10″. Des Moines Art Center. 211

22.4. Rembrandt Harmensz. van Rijn: *Abraham Caressing Isaac* (ca. 1637). Etching, 4⅝″ × 3½″. Des Moines Art Center. 211

22.5. Theo van Rysselberghe: *Marie Sethe at the Piano* (1891). Conte crayon, 12½″ × 14⅛″. Art Institute of Chicago. 213

22.6. A student drawing using crosshatch. Black and white pencil on construction paper. 214

22.7. A student drawing using crosshatch. Black and white pencil on construction paper. 214

23.1. A student drawing showing the use of values stroked over geometric volumes in a landscape. Charcoal on white drawing paper. 217

23.2. A student drawing showing the use of values kept as planes. Charcoal on charcoal paper. 218

23.3. A student drawing showing the use of values stroked over geometric volumes in a landscape. Graphite on white drawing paper. 218

23.4. Pieter Brueghel the Elder: *Haymaking (July)* (1565). Oils on oak, 46¹¹⁄₁₆″ × 63⅜″. National Gallery, Prague. 219

23.5. Rodolphe Bresdin: *Le Grand Arbre Noir* (ca. 1860). Ink on tracing paper, 26″ × 18⅛″. Gemeentemuseum, The Hague. 220

23.6. Wayne Thiebaud: *Landscape* (1965). Pencil, 9″ × 12″. Allan Stone Galleries, New York. 220

23.7. William Zimmerman: *Icy Fingers* (1973). Acrylic, 5″ × 7″. 221

24.1. Linear composition. 227

24.2. Geometric-shapes composition. 227

24.3. Sight-lines composition. 229

24.4. Value-shapes composition. 229

26.1. Rodolphe Bresdin: *The Flight into Egypt* (1855). Lithograph, 22¼″ × 17½″. 248

26.2. Giovanni Domenico Tiepolo: *The Holy Family Passing under an Arch* (ca. 1750–1755). Etching, 7¼″ × 9⅝″. Private collection. 249

27.1. Ed Ruscha and Kenneth Price: *Frog and Flies* (1969). Color lithograph, 23⅛″ × 34″. Des Moines Art Center. 256

27.2. René Magritte: *The Thought Which Sees* (1965). Graphite, 15¾″ × 11⅝″. Museum of Modern Art, New York. 257

27.3. Student drawing using repetition of images. Graphite on white drawing paper. 258

27.4. Student drawing using repetition of images. Charcoal and chalk on charcoal paper. 258

27.5. Student drawing using repetition of images. Ink on white drawing paper. 258

28.1. Student composition of selected shapes and objects. Charcoal on charcoal paper. 262

List of Illustrations

28.2. Student composition of selected shapes and objects. Charcoal on charcoal paper. 262

29.1. Pablo Picasso: *Ambroise Vollard* (1909–1910). Oil on canvas, 36″ × 26½″. Pushkin Museum, Moscow. 264

29.2. Georges Braque: *The Portuguese* (1911). Oil on canvas, 46⅛″ × 32″. Offentliche Kunstsammlung, Basel. 265

29.3. Pablo Picasso: *Still Life with Chair Caning* (1911–1912). Paint and pasted oil cloth simulating chair caning, 10½″ × 13¾″, oval. Collection, the artist. 266

29.4. A student composition using mixed media (brown paper bag, charcoal, and ink). 267

29.5. A student composition using mixed media (brown paper bag, newspaper, and charcoal). 267

29.6. A student composition using mixed media (brown paper bag, chalk, and ink). 268

29.7. A student composition using mixed media (brown paper bag, newspaper, graphite, and ink). 268

30.1. W. Woolett after William Hogarth: *Satire on False Perspective,* frontispiece to Kirby's *Perspective of Architecture* (1761). Engraving. Museum of Fine Arts, Boston. 271

30.2. Salvador Dali: *Crucifixion* (1951). Oil on canvas, 80⅝″ × 40⅝″. Glasgow Art Gallery and Museum. 272

30.3. Two-point perspective, plan view and perspective view. 274

30.4. One-point perspective, plan view and perspective view A. 278

30.5. One-point perspective, plan view and perspective view B. 281

30.6. Three-point perspective, plan view, perspective view, and elevation. 285

30.7. Student drawing in cross contour. 286

30.8. Student composition using an eraser as the drawing tool. 288

30.9. Student drawing using the fewest lines and shapes to identify subject matter (chair, reeds, birdcage, drapery, and bamboo screen). 289

30.10. Student drawing using the fewest lines and shapes to identify subject matter (a pig's head). 289

30.11. Student drawing using the fewest lines and shapes to identify subject matter (female nude, seen from behind, seated on material). 290

30.12. Student drawing using the fewest lines and shapes to identify subject matter (girl leaning against chair). 290

31.1. Steps in matting: plastic right angle, pencil, dot. 296

31.2. Steps in matting: free hand behind blade. 298

31.3. Steps in matting: tape drawing, oaktag. 300

31.4. Steps in matting: frame, acetate, drawing, oaktag. 300

31.5. Steps in matting: 1½-inch strips of cloth tape, drawing, backing board. 302

31.6. Steps in matting: ruler, acetate, miter. 303

31.7. Steps in matting: taped acetate pulled to back. 303

31.8. Steps in matting: hinge 3-inch tape at corners.   304

31.9. Rembrandt Harmensz. van Rijn: *Self-Portrait* (1659). Canvas, 33¼″ × 26″. National Gallery of Art, Washington, D.C.   307

COLOR PLATES

Color plates follow page 216

I.   Rogier van der Weyden: *The Descent from the Cross* (ca. 1435). Panel, 7′ 2⅝″ × 8′ 7⅛″. Prado, Madrid.

II.   Color-shapes composition.

III. Raphael: *The Miraculous Draught of Fishes* (1515–1516). Cartoon, gouache on paper, 141″ × 168″. Victoria and Albert Museum, London.

IV.   Albrecht Dürer: *Adam and Eve* (1504). Copperplate engraving, 10″ × 7½″. Museum of Fine Arts, Boston.

V.   Peter Paul Rubens: *The Defeat of Sennacherib* (1616–1618). Oil on canvas, 3′ 2⅝″ × 4′ ⅜″. Alte Pinakothek, Munich.

VI.   Pierre-Auguste Renoir: *Le Moulin de la Galette* (1876). Oil, 51½″ × 69″. Louvre, Paris.

VII. Pierre-Paul Prud'hon: *La Source* (ca. 1801). Black and white chalk, 21 3/16″ × 15 5/16″. Sterling and Francine Clark Art Institute, Williamstown, Massachusetts.

VIII. Rembrandt Harmensz. van Rijn: *Female Nude Seated and Bending Forward* (1660–1662). India ink and bistre wash, 11¼″ × 6 5/16″. British Museum, London.

IX.   Richard Lindner: *Hello* (1966). Oil on canvas, 70″ × 60″. Private collection, New York.

X.   Francis Bacon: *Head Surrounded by Sides of Beef* (1954). Oil on canvas, 50⅞″ × 48″. Art Institute of Chicago.

XI.   James Ensor: *The Artist's Father in Death* (1887). Pencil, black crayon, opaque white on brown paper, 6¾″ × 9″. Private collection.

XII. James Ensor: *The Artist's Father in Death* (1887). Conte crayon. Koninklijk Museum, Antwerp.

PREFACE

For the two decades during which I have been drawing and painting with greatest seriousness, I have never had what most working artists would regard as a "studio," that bright, spacious, professional environment similar to the well-preserved one Rubens enjoyed. I have moved supplies and models variously from flooded basements to apartment kitchens, from collapsing tailgates to unheated garages, from temporary alcoves to what once seemed a permanent consignment in a boiler room. Ultimately, for me studio has come to mean a state of mind as much as place. Studio is where the job gets done.

Most students who use this book will do so in a studio classroom. Good classrooms can develop good rhythms: the daily—or, at the least, semiweekly—setup of materials and assignments, the *doing,* the repeated undertaking of spatial translations, increasingly complex and often tested by the person sitting alongside. At some point the best studio classroom will itself translate into a state of mind. The external motivations become internal ones, and a drawing habitat will be in whatever room you find yourself.

For those few students who are "on their own" with this book—not a recommended route—I must caution that the exercises are with few exceptions interdependent and cumulative. A too casual, random selection of projects will be betrayed in your work. Sometimes one or two drawing applications can be privately mastered, at least superficially. But such success is disarmingly inhibiting. It can serve to keep you from seeing your shortcomings. Your images may suddenly seem "real" enough, even "pretty," but will actually have about the same authority a well-memorized phrase has to the sensitive uses of a foreign language. Drawing is a way of thinking about space. It requires the same careful ordering of assumptions, evidence, and logic found in any good thinking, all the while coexisting with spontaneous creative leaps. Any new vocabulary of expectations and responses needs time to settle in.

How much time? Either in class or privately the student should view these exercises as comprising a ten- to sixteen-week program. A drawing teacher will quickly recognize the standard components of a one-term course. Such a term allows the student both a compressed rehearsal of preliminary skills and a reasonable gestation for personal discovery. In most artistic disciplines the simplest applications tend to be very transparent in their achievement, or lack thereof, and students will return frequently, for years, to fundamentals. But at this stage a student should aim to appropriate one comprehensive body of fundamentals.

In a school, typically, *studio* is the word for those activities that stress the practical nuts-and-bolts, firsthand methods of an art form, as distinct from its more theoretical or historical concerns. This book tries to minimize the distinction. An attempt is made to integrate practice, theory, and history at each step. I am aware of perils in that attempt. In the narrow scope of this book historical material is sometimes anecdotal, and theory is often reduced to a strategically posed question. But my experience has been that students thrive on learning of the traditions and the ancestral experiments in their study. Students rarely let ignorance or modesty stand in the way of asking tough questions. When a student inquires whether line itself is the subject of a drawing, is simply autographic, or is the essence of form, much can be gained from pausing in a speculative byway for a while. Shared discourse can often yield productive clues otherwise missing in the mere contemplation of a bowl of fruit.

Wayne Thiebaud (b. 1920, American): *Toys* (1971). Charcoal on paper, 20″ × 26″. Collection, the artist.

In two respects theory and history are treated more informatively. First, the material on perspective is uncomplicated and—in terms of linear perspective—comprehensive in an introductory sense. Second, the criticism activities attached to this beginning drawing course are here provided with a detailed methodology. Students are often pressed to visit galleries and to view masterworks, but then find themselves sorely underequipped for developing a critical position. This book does have at least one clear functional hook for the beginning analyst/artist.

One final word about hooks and handles and rules in general. Use them as they come your way. Time-honored procedures should not be casually discarded. Art in the Renaissance was an intellectual, scientific, and poetic discipline. Draftsmanship was of first importance, though drawing played a service role to painting, sculpture, and architecture. Only in the last two hundred years have artists viewed themselves as originators of a mystery called Art, capital *A*, with drawing emerging from its "adjunct" role into a major expressive medium in its own right.

But contemporary drawing has returned to classical roots for re-definition. Classical roots have standards and precepts. Follow that route, and you'll learn soon enough which exceptions prove the rules.

ACKNOWLEDGMENTS

Rare is the textbook that surfaces without the forebearance, willing or unwilling, of students. For providing illustrative works, I am able to credit a few students by name in the back of the book. But hundreds more could join that list in their responsibility for supplying the tough questions and the communication tests that drove this visually oriented person to her typewriter. Mention must be made in the front of the book of two former students whose imprint is more singular. Brian Wolf posed and proposed for the section on matting. Kevin Scott mastered the task of bringing graphic clarity to complex information by drawing the perspective illustrations.

Inevitably, there are colleagues whose expertise one needs, and I have leaned on a few in the hallways of Iowa State University. William Zimmerman tracked historical data and challenged my premises with friendly, persistent vigor. Ron Fenimore unscrambled my confusions on typeface, layout, and design. John Weinkein and Larry Ferguson read the manuscript in its early stages and offered helpful comment. Lyman Greiner was most patient with my often uncertain photographic objectives.

Many friends, including writer John Martin, teachers Karen Pinter and Gerald Gedekes, local businessman Max LaBlanc, and Renaissance neighbor Jette Foss, advanced and tested principles. Such folks were also forthright goads toward the clarifying of murky prose.

The following academic reviewers have rendered special and manifold assistance: Vincent J. Bruno, University of Texas, Arlington; A. Robert Birmelin, Queens College of the City University of New York; Robert William McCarter, North Texas State University; June P. Magaziner, Bronx Community College; Richard M. Proctor, University of Washington; Larry Ferguson, Iowa State University.

Special thanks go to Sam Carini, assistant curator of prints and drawings for the Art Institute of Chicago, to Peggy Patrick, assistant director of the Des Moines Art Center, and to her assistant, Euphemia Connor, for generous access to files, private collections, and knowledgeable tips.

Vicky Bice, with secretarial acumen as much in her head as in her capable fingers, helped see me through more than one deadline.

Last of all, I salute the two editors in my life: H. Stafford Bryant, Jr., whose kindly, professional guidance focused matters during the long final processes; and Andrew, my husband, without whose strategic editing and playful ratiocination the book might have been completed sooner. And prematurely.

Drawing

A STUDIO GUIDE

Part One

INTRODUCTION

I

STARTING: PROCESS
AND MEDIA

This book is for the beginning art student, for the person who wants to draw and who wants a plan to follow.

Whatever the field you intend as an artist—fine arts, advertising design, crafts, architecture, landscape architecture—your primary instincts for selections of space will be serviced by drawing. From the discipline of translating three dimensions into two dimensions you will discover both a gradual refinement and a personalization in the uses of space. These discoveries can transfer to buildings, paintings, jewelry, sculpture, scenery, fabrics, furniture, prints, mosaics—what you will.

The importance of spending months on the fundamentals of drawing may not be obvious immediately. Repetition unavoidably is a key. Repeated acts of seeing, selecting, and thinking through the physical marking on paper are indispensable to growth. Reading about art or talking about drawing will not do what pencil in hand will do.

The problems in this book are devised to give room to work in your own way, using your distinctive capabilities. If you feel you do not understand precisely what to do, keep trying. Drawing takes repeated effort. Moments of insight will come *as you are working*.

Working in your own way is your best approach to a solution to a problem. A guide can give you experienced challenges by way of exercises, subject matter, and materials.

Indeed, the spatial resolutions, the subjects, and the materials are, in a Gestalt, the sum components of what can become a work of art. The difference between a doodle and a sensitive drawing, between a splatter and a master painting hangs upon matters of significant form. But at the outset, a great deal of technical discipline must usually come before creative leaps succeed. Technical discipline is the thrust of this book. The primary activity is the act of drawing, of finding repeated solutions to spatial problems. Along the way, however, there are distractions to avoid.

On occasion you will feel blocked and frustrated, and instead of the discipline of drawing, you may seek different subject matter to prod you to better work. Resist the temptation. Only when you become absorbed in solving the problem rather than in escaping to a new venture are you on your way to serious drawing.

Another temptation is copying. Virtual copies are frequently seen in works by students whose primary concern is to be correct. As an illustration, see Figure 1.1.

This young man drew the profile of a bone and colored it in. For a bone drawing it "looks good." But this student's ability to draw was severely limited because he could not comprehend what to do beyond copying lighting effects.

A second student, a young woman, was on a more substantive path toward solutions (see Figure 1.2), figuring first the compositional layout, then working with line, letting it play over the planes of the bones, feeling her way with her eyes, groping for information intrinsic to the skeleton. Translating information about the total space, using both positive shapes (things) and negative shapes (space that permeates or surrounds things), she drew with sensitive line and value.

A third distraction students sometimes fall into is adopting a superficial technique used to produce an effect. Many students want the end product at the start. That is, they want the picture they produce to look professional, as if it had been drawn by an "artist." This book is not intended as a short course in performance. It is planned to promote long-range growth. Should you latch upon a flashy technique

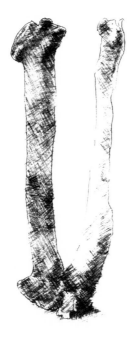

FIGURE 1.1. Bone drawing as a virtual copy.

FIGURE 1.2. Bone drawing with composition in mind.

too early in your work, you are likely to lose a great deal of integrity and individualism in expression. You may begin drawing everything the same way, in which case your capacity for thinking through problems becomes an exercise in technical redundancy. Any method extracted and used as "the" way to draw quickly becomes a technique void of meaning. Let what you see, not what you think about drawings you have seen, dictate your stroke. Therein lies the discipline in drawing. Study the problem, draw, learn in the process. Drawing is a motor/visual event that requires problem solving through your uniqueness. The problems are given. *You* can solve them.

The subject matter used in these processes is traditional—the still life, the landscape, the figure. Exercises in this book accommodate that subject matter with progressive difficulty. Traditional subject matter does allow you a variety of experiences with space. A still life usually suggests a close, contained space, while a landscape reaches toward infinity. Traditional subject matters will serve you well until you find spatial concerns that may or may not include them.

Rather than detailing the almost endless range of marketed art supplies, our discussion of media and materials will be related only to the drawing supplies you will use during the course of this book.

Lines, values, and colors are produced by media stroked on a surface or support, whether it is a wall or a sheet of paper. Media have dry, wet, or grease bases. Paper, the customary support, varies also. The variables are "tooth," quality, color, size, and type.

PAPERS

Tooth refers to the roughness of the surface characterized by different finishes. Cold-Pressed papers (designated CP) and papers not pressed are more coarse in texture than the Hot-Pressed papers (designated HP), which are generally smooth. Quality usually refers to the rag content and the weight of the paper. Pounds per ream or grams per square meter indicate weight. Heavier, rougher papers are used more for water-base media because of absorbency; however, many such papers are used for dry or grease-base media. Sizes range from small sheets, individual or bound, to large rolls. The type or character of the paper depends on the kind of fiber used—linen, flax, cotton, wood, hemp, and so on. Type also refers to the process—machine-made, hand-made, or a combination of those methods.

A paper product designated as 100-percent rag is made entirely of cloth rags, usually of cotton or linen fibers. Papers with less than 100-percent rag content are combinations of rag, wood pulp, and chemicals. The acids used to disintegrate the wood are never fully washed out, and the residue causes papers to yellow. However, papers made from wood are more economically produced than 100-percent rag papers, which can be three to five times as expensive.

Rags of cotton or linen do not require harsh chemicals for breaking down fibers. The 100-percent rag papers remain relatively neutral (nonyellowing), although sizings (fillers such as alum or rosin) are used, and contain some chemicals that produce acids that degrade the paper. Usually, yellowing is at a minimum or nonexistent in the 100-percent rag papers.

Any papers with dyes in them have a high acidic content. For that reason, white or natural off-white papers and mats are better for long-term use (see Figure 1.3).

Most of the papers used for beginning work are made from wood pulp simply because using them is less expensive and much of the work will be discarded. Later, your more refined sensibilities and the uses of superior papers will go hand in hand. Each will make a demand on the other. When you make a stroke on newsprint and a stroke on 100-percent rag paper and know what the difference means, then you are ready to take the costlier risks.

Amount

2–3 18″ × 24″ smooth newsprint pads (the cheapest stock drawing paper)

4–6 single sheets of smooth white drawing paper

2–4 sheets of oaktag, Manila or white

2–3 sheets of white or cream charcoal paper

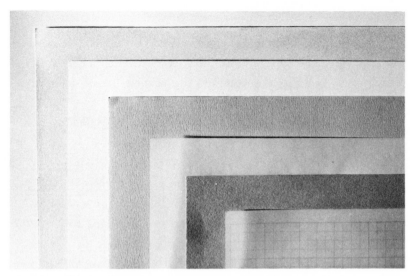

FIGURE 1.3. Kinds of paper.

3–5 sheets of middle-tone charcoal papers such as blue, green, or
   gray (Charcoal paper has a fairly rough tooth.)

8 sheets of tracing papers

2 sheets of middle-tone construction paper, such as blue, green,
   or gray

PENCILS

Raw graphite, a form of crystallized carbon, was first discovered in Eng-
land about 1560. The natural mineral varied considerably in hardness.
Two centuries later N. J. Conté patented a pencil-making process per-
mitting quality control. Pencil cores were made of graphite mixed
with clay, then fired or baked. The hardened cores were inserted into
hollow cylinders of wood. Harder cores had more clay, soft cores, less
(see Figure 1.4).

Manufacturers now use a synthetic graphite that can be dark or light,
fine or coarse, hard or soft. The H lettering from 2 to 6 indicates
increasingly harder cores. The B lettering from 2 to 6 indicates increasingly softer cores. Softer pencil cores need care in sharpening.
Slowly rotating the handle of a pencil sharpener should prevent the
breaking of points.

Graphite produces shades of gray. Colored pencils are mixtures of pigment pastes and binders, also manufactured with hard or soft cores.

Amount
1   2H pencil
3   2B pencils
1   3B, 4B, and 6B pencil
1   box of colored pencils
1   black colored pencil ⎱ if neither of these is in the
1   white colored pencil ⎰ box of colored pencils

CHARCOAL, CHALK, AND CRAYONS

Vine charcoal is usually derived from birch, willow, or berry vines burned to carbon. Since no binders are added to vine charcoal, it is

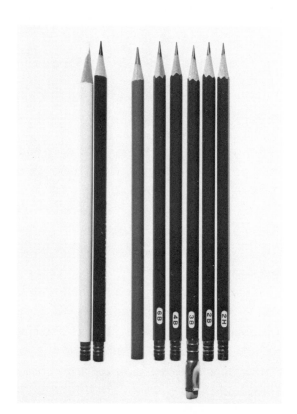

FIGURE 1.4. Kinds of pencils.

soft, breaks easily and yields mild intensities. Unless vine charcoal drawings are "fixed" with a spray fixative, the charcoal will rub off easily. Compressed charcoal, which is pulverized charcoal with a binding agent added, is formed into sticks. As a drawing implement, a compressed charcoal stick yields rich, dense blacks. Carbon pencils are simply compressed charcoal encased in wood. Sharpening charcoal pencils should be done with extreme care. The cores are soft and break easily. Powdered pigment materials mixed with a binder (and with more or less oil or wax) and compressed into a stick, will give you chalk (less oil) or crayon (more oil). Charcoal, chalk, and crayon tend to work better on paper with a fairly rough tooth. These media vary from dry to greasy, coarse to fine, and hard to soft (see Figure 1.5).

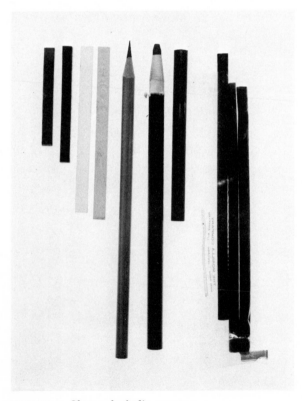

FIGURE 1.5. Charcoal, chalk, crayons.

Amount

1	package vine charcoal
1–2	cylindrical sticks of compressed charcoal
1–2	charcoal pencils (optional)
1	carbon pencil (BB and optional)
1	gray chalk
1	white chalk
2	black conte crayons
1	litho crayon (optional)

ERASERS

Two of the earliest erasers were vanes of feathers and crumbs of bread. The importation of caoutchouc (pronounced kōō chŏŏk), the elastic residue from a milky substance in tropical plants, effected an eraser better than bread crumbs. Caoutchouc was the prototype of our current eraser, which is vulcanized (by adding heat and chemicals) to impart greater elasticity, durability, or hardness.

Many of today's erasers use petroleum by-products. The synthetic eraser is soft enough not to damage paper and crumbles gradually when used. An eraser that does not crumble will only smear.

The "kneaded" eraser is used primarily to erase large areas of charcoal. When kneaded with your fingers, the eraser self-cleans to some degree, and can be used again and again (see Figure 1.6).

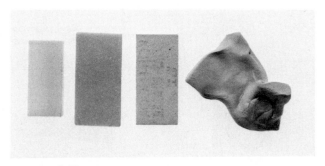

FIGURE 1.6. Erasers.

Amount

1 synthetic eraser
1 kneaded eraser

INK AND BRUSHES

India ink, made from lampblack or carbon, has a dense but fluid consistency. It is waterproof because a shellac binder is mixed with the pigment. India ink quickly absorbs colors mixed with it and for that reason toning colored inks with India ink should be done carefully. Linear work done with ink flows well on a smooth, hard paper. Wash drawings using a brush with ink work better on a softer, more absorbent paper.

Brushes vary from coarse bristle to soft sable. Brushes are made with flat or round and short or long tufts, which in turn have different ends—pointed, rounded, or square. Brushes are numbered according to the width of the tuft. Round sable brushes, called Rounds, are best for our purposes (see Figure 1.7).

FIGURE 1.7. Ink and brushes.

Starting: Process and Media

Amount

1   bottle of India ink
1   bottle of white ink
1   bottle of middle-dark ink, such as sepia (brown) blue, green, etc.
2   brushes, 1 large and 1 medium or small
3   small bottles (such as small jars for mixing inks)

PENS

Historically, artists have used four basic types of pens—quill pens cut from feathers, reed pens cut from bamboo or cane, metal pens, and felt- or nylon-tip pens.

The best quill pens are made from the feathers of a goose, a swan, a raven, or a crow. Of these, the goose quill seems to be the most popular because of its versatility and gliding capabilities.

Reed pens predate quills but were usually too blunt for the delicate work often seen in illuminated manuscripts. Even today the width, thickness, and fibrousness of the reed points seem less responsive in the hands of artists than other pens. Both the quill and reed pen points need to be cut, shaped, and prepared before use.

Metal pens are ready to use when you purchase them. And pens of nearly every type, including technical pens or pens with felt or nylon tips, are available in art stores. Metal points bought to insert into a holder are sometimes covered with a light varnish for protection. Should you purchase such points, hold them under warm running water to dissolve the shellac. The most serviceable pen for our problems is the nylon razor-tip pen (see Figure 1.8).

Amount

1   nylon razor-tip pen
1   technical pen (optional)
1   holder (optional)
1   each of 5-B and 6-B Speedball points (optional)
assorted felt tips (optional)

FIGURE 1.8. Pens.

Assorted Supplies

Amount

2	pounds of plasticene clay (an oil-based clay)
1	small cork or styrofoam ball
4	toothpicks
5	mat boards, 30″ × 40″ (white/off-white or white/gray)
	assorted acetate
7″–12″	of cloth tape, nonacidic
1	small roll brown paper tape
1	small roll masking tape
1	12″ ruler
1	metal yardstick
1	protractor
1	can fixative
1	sandpaper block (for sharpening charcoal)
1	drawing board (optional)
1	black portfolio (20″ × 26″)
1	tool kit or fishing tackle box for supplies

Before using any tool new to you, work with it on several kinds of paper with a loose, free manipulation. Keep discarded drawings and other scraps of paper for testing media. Test the "drag" or pull of the pencil, the conte crayon, the chalk; in your hand each will feel quite different. As you work through the exercises, your experience with media and materials will inform you of the limitations and potentials of the ones you do use.

FIGURE 1.9. Mat boards.

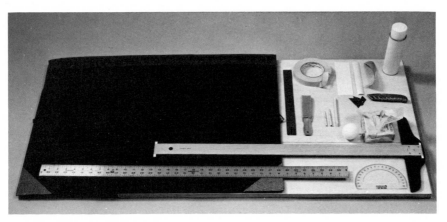

FIGURE 1.10. Assorted supplies.

Part Two

───────

THE
CONTOUR LINE

FIGURE 2.1. Hans Holbein the Younger (1497–1543, German): *The Family of Sir Thomas More* (1526). Pen and ink, 15⁷⁄₁₆″ × 20¼″. Offentliche Kunstsammlung, Basel.

FIGURE 2.2. Philipp Otto Runge (1777–1810, German): *Lily with Hovering Genii* (1809). Pen and ink, 26½″ × 17¹¹⁄₁₆″. Kunsthalle, Hamburg.

FIGURE 2.3. Henri Matisse (1869–1954, French): *Reclining Nude* (1937). Charcoal, 15″ × 19″. Art Institute of Chicago.

FIGURE 2.4. Pablo Picasso (1881–1973, Spanish): study for the painting *Pipes of Pan* (ca. 1923). Charcoal, 25¾₁₆″ × 19⁵₁₆″. Art Institute of Chicago.

FIGURE 2.5. Jean-Auguste-Dominique Ingres (1780–1867, French): *Charles-François Mallet, Civil Engineer* (1809). Pencil, 10⁹⁄₁₆″ × 8⅜″. Art Institute of Chicago.

FIGURE 2.6. Hans Holbein the Younger (1497–1543, German): *Portrait of Frau Burgermeister Dorothea Meyer* (ca. 1535). Colored chalk, 15⅜″ × 11″. Museum Faesch, Basel.

FIGURE 2.7. Katsushika Hokusai (1760–1846, Japanese): *Self-Portrait* (ca. 1845). Brush and ink. Musée Guimet, Paris.

FIGURE 2.8. John L. Weinkein (b. 1941, American): *Great-Grandfather* (1977). Colored pencil, 20″ × 24″. Private Collection.

2

BLIND CONTOUR AND
BALANCE IN COMPOSITION

TOOLS
2B or 3B pencil
newsprint

Drawing is translating. What you first perceive in three dimensions is encoded in your mind's eye and finally deciphered into your form of visual communication.

The process of learning how to translate consists of exercises in seeing, in deciphering, and in image making. Drawing is a simultaneous, many-layered discipline that moves the student toward a distinctive artistic perception in the organization of space. With practice, your eye will teach your hand and your hand will teach your eye.

The earliest and simplest method of drawing was delineation. Its most pure form is the contour line. The contour line is the demarking of what is there and what is not. The contour is the boundary between what is perceived, called the positive shape, and the space surrounding the perceived object, called the negative shape. The impact of a well-drawn contour line rests in sensitive and persuasive information. It is a deceptively difficult line to draw well.

The first-century Roman encyclopedist, Pliny the Elder, observed the difficulty. "An artist is rarely successful in finding an outline which

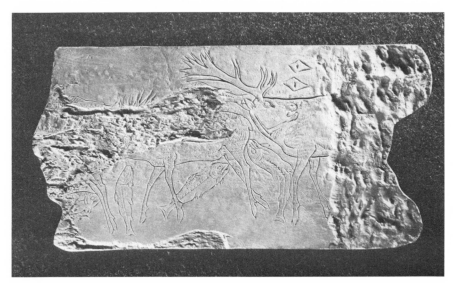

FIGURE 2.9. *Stags (or Reindeer) Crossing a Stream with Fish* (prehistoric). Impression rolled from an engraved staff, a reindeer antler, 9¾″ long, Lortet (Hautes-Pyrénées), France. Musée des Antiquités Nationales, Saint-Germaine-en-Laye.

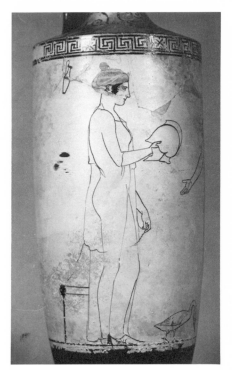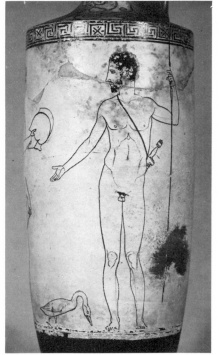

FIGURE 2.10. The Achilles Painter: white-ground lekythos (ca. 440 B.C.). Pottery, 15″ high. British Museum, London.

Blind Contour and Balance

shall express the contours of the figure. For the contour should appear to fold back and so enclose the object as to give assurance of the parts behind, thus clearly suggesting even what it conceals." [1]

Pliny's admonishment notwithstanding, outlines have been of primary interest to artists for centuries, including the earliest cave dwellers, ca. 15,000 B.C. (see Figure 2.9), the Greek pottery artisans, ca. 420 B.C. (see Figure 2.10), and Pablo Picasso, A.D. 1921 (see Figure 2.11).

In our first assignment, we need something with less complex information than the full figure for subject matter. Let's start by taking a look at your finger, an object in space only an arm's length away.

Sit for a minute or two and study the topside profile of the surface distance between your wrist and the tip of your forefinger. Even though you have lived with your finger longer than anyone else, you may be surprised how little you know about it. There is highly individualized information here, much like the personal idiosyncracies of a finger-

FIGURE 2.11. Pablo Picasso (1881–1973, Spanish): *La Source* (1921). Pencil, 19″ × 25¼″. Museum of Modern Art, New York.

print. Now, how do you translate that information into line? You need to develop a seeing hand by committing an act of faith. Keep your eyes off the paper. Trust your hand.

Look only at the span between the wrist and the tip of your index finger on the hand not holding the pencil. Look again. Concentrate. Observe slowly, until nothing exists except that boundary, wrist to finger, containing information about bumps, knicks, indentations, hair, warts, what have you. Spend three minutes drawing that arbitrary line alone, moving your eye only as fast as your pencil moves, proceeding slowly, keeping your pencil on the paper, remembering that the line defines the positive from the negative. You are drawing "blind contour" (see Figures 2.12 and 2.13).

Quality in visual information is necessary. You need to see as much as possible. Generally speaking, the slower you go the more informative will be your translation. Imagine the pencil touching your hand as you draw. Draw as much honest information as you can observe. Draw all that is there.

If you draw quickly, the line can be uninteresting and not much information is transmitted. A line drawn something like this ⌒ , is a line largely barren of information.

Draw slowly now for three minutes, one line, wrist to finger.

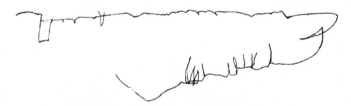

FIGURE 2.12. Student drawing, wrist to finger, in blind contour. Pencil on newsprint.

FIGURE 2.13. Student drawing, wrist to finger, in blind contour. Pencil on newsprint.

FIGURE 2.14. Student drawing of a hand in blind contour. Pencil on newsprint.

FIGURE 2.15. Student drawing of a hand in blind contour. Pencil on newsprint.

For your second drawing, repeat the contour process with another portion of your hand, trying two or three fingers (see Figures 2.14 and 2.15). Hold your hand in such a way that it will not begin to shake—place it on the table, hold it against a lamp, whatever. Again, look at the hand only, and draw slowly. Make this blind contour study a five-minute exercise. Keep your eyes on the hand, not on the paper, moving your eyes at the same very slow speed you move your pencil.

The aim of blind contour is to make your perception more discriminating. Don't anticipate that your drawing should look like a copy of what you see. Remember, you are deciphering the code in your mind's eye. At this stage, work for a sensitive, informed line, not a tracing.

Draw slowly for five minutes, using any section of the hand.

Next, draw one of your shoes for a ten-minute study. First, remove it. Most persons will place their shoe in functional positions, sole flat. They are thinking functionally, not aesthetically. What points of view can you handle with that shoe? Are you looking at it from the top? Straight on? From the sole? Twisted with the tongue hanging out? The laces gone?

By squashing, bending, or opening the shoe, you can produce a more interesting shape; hence, a more interesting drawing (see Figures 2.16 and 2.17).

Move into the shoe itself for more information—e.g., the stitching, texture, eyelets, laces—but keep your eyes on the shoe, not the paper. Eyelets may be drawn misplaced, laces suspended in space, or stitching to the side of the shoe, but remember, at this stage, it is the quality of the line found in descriptive information through seeing that's important. Keep your eyes on the shoe. Get enough information about the shoe into your line so that the line you draw speaks uniquely about that shoe and about the point of view you have chosen.

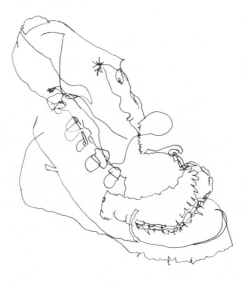

FIGURE 2.16. Student drawing of a shoe in blind contour. Pencil on newsprint.

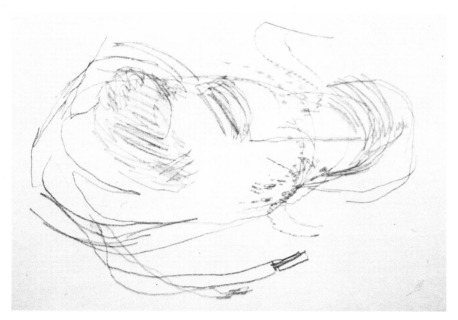

FIGURE 2.17. Student drawing of a shoe in blind contour. Pencil on newsprint.

A profile is the next step. A model or a neighboring student will do. With a large folding mirror, you might draw your own.

As you sit to the side of the person, first studying the profile, forehead to brow, to nose, to lip, to chin, try to realize the line drawn of that profile also separates that portion of the head from the space it displaces.

Once again, observe deliberately until nothing exists except that boundary containing information unique to that individual—bumps, indentations, proportions, curves.

Slowly, for five minutes, draw a life-sized blind contour of the profile before you (see Figures 2.18 and 2.19).

For more practice with line you might move now to a subject farther away (see Figure 2.20), repeating the same procedure, always keeping your eye off the paper, constantly appraising characteristics to draw in the line, using the length of time you feel you need. You might want to try doing a still life, a portion of a room, a person who will sit for you. (Warn your model that it is not a portrait and is likely to be somewhat unflattering.)

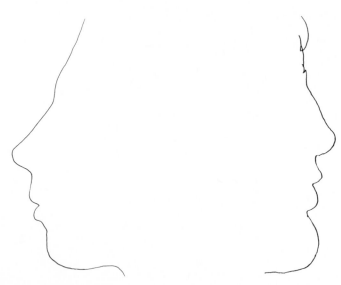

FIGURE 2.18. Student drawing of a profile in blind contour. Pencil on white drawing paper.

FIGURE 2.19. Student drawing of a profile in blind contour. Pencil on white drawing paper.

Another form of blind contour is drawing through your sense of touch.

If you can, find an object with a fairly obvious surface texture—a piece of driftwood, an ear of corn, a corduroy jacket. Smooth objects are less instructive than textured objects.

Close your eyes, and as you feel your way down, across, around, up, and over, draw a line that indicates your tactile impressions. You will discover that you can vary the impression of the object through the pressure of your pencil—by pressing harder when a portion of the object recedes and pressing less hard when a portion of the object protrudes. This pressure varies, if but subtly, the lights and darks in your line, tending to produce a more expressive line than does a solid, non-varied, lead-gray line (see Figures 2.21 and 2.22).

Again, draw carefully. Draw conscientiously. Feel with your eyes closed. Draw slowly as you touch your way over the object.

When you have finished this problem, tape your work on a wall and study it for a while.

Note how you have used the total space, the whole sheet of paper.

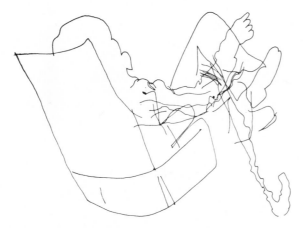

FIGURE 2.20. Student drawing of a model in a chair in blind contour. Pencil on newsprint.

FIGURE 2.21. Student drawing of a felt contour. Pencil on newsprint.

FIGURE 2.22. Student drawing of a felt contour. Pencil on newsprint.

Where is your drawing placed? To the left, right, middle? Does it run off the edges?

Since you were drawing "blind" you might be perplexed at the question. I am asking you how well your spatial instincts worked. Your sheet of paper is a piece of space with fixed boundaries on which you draw something. Each time you draw a line, you divide that whole space, and you will discover that some divisions are more pleasing than others.

Composition is essentially integrated spatial organization, which is a complex artistic concern, and difficult to define precisely. Composition will be discussed throughout this study in different contexts in order to give broad exposure to its full meaning, but it is well to note at the outset that there are no hard and fast rules. Good compositions will result from judgments that mature in cumulative studio experiences and from your extensive viewing of good art.

Because growth in solving studio problems develops with growth in composing, some facility with traditional concepts of composition is encouraged. The immediate concern is to develop rule-of-thumb guidelines for decisions you need to make continuously while drawing. Eventually, these decisions should become instinctive ones. Composition in a drawing or painting is at bottom simply the interplay of line, shape, value, and color. Whenever these elements are applied with sensitivity and skill, a pleasing composition will result.

What is traditionally pleasing in a composition? Balance is part of the answer. Shapes will impart "weight" depending on their placement on the sheet, on their gradations in color or value, and on their relationship to other shapes. If the weights are distributed comfortably, or proportionately, or rhythmically, or surprisingly, some kind of pleasure will probably result.

Balance is usually described as formal (symmetrical) or informal (asymmetrical). Formal or informal balance helps describe eye movement to, within, and around a *center of interest*—that is, where the main focus of the work lies.

One solution for deriving a center of interest for informal balance is

FIGURE 2.23. Albrecht Altdorfer (ca. 1480–1538, Bavarian): *Battle of Alexander* (1529). Lime panel, 62¼″ × 47¼″. Alte Pinakothek, Munich.

based on divisions of thirds. If a rectangle is divided into thirds with lines, horizontal and vertical, any of the points of intersection can become a center of interest. The solution for formal balance is even simpler: the center of interest rests somewhere on the vertical center line of your rectangle.

Keeping a center of interest in mind, the artist works to influence eye movement toward that area. Verticals, horizontals, or diagonals combined with value contrasts, colors, and shapes should serve to move the viewer into the composition and to the area of greatest importance (see Figure 2.23).

The illusion of depth is called perspective. Lines that render perspective will tend to move the eye swiftly to a specific point. Linear perspective is the most formal means of establishing relative size from foreground to background (see Figure 2.24).

Aerial perspective renders depth through the diffusion of colors, val-

FIGURE 2.24. Johannes Bosboom (1819–1891): church interior (ca. 1860). Water color and gouache over pencil, 16⅛″ × 12¼″. Art Institute of Chicago.

FIGURE 2.25. Joseph Mallord William Turner (1775–1851, English): *The Slave Ship* (1840). Oil painting, 35¾″ × 48″. Museum of Fine Arts, Boston.

ues, and textures from foreground to background (see Figure 2.25). (We will deal with perspective in greater detail in Chapter Eight.)

If the artist places us behind the head of someone looking into the scene, we feel we are there too, almost standing within the composition (see Figure 2.26).

If the artist draws a figure whose gaze is straight to the viewer, the device arrests us, as if the stranger stared us into sharing his space (see Figure 2.27).

Once a viewer is within a composition, the eye should stay there, moving within and around the center of interest, not drifting too far

FIGURE 2.26. Heinrich Voegler: *Eine Liebe* ("*A Love*") (1896). Etching, 13¾″ × 14⅞″. Des Moines Art Center.

FIGURE 2.27. John Singer Sargent (1856–1925, American): *The Pailleron Children* (1881). Oil painting, 60″ × 69″. Des Moines Art Center.

FIGURE 2.28. Raffaello Sanzio, known as Raphael (1483–1520, Italian): *Baldassare Castiglione* (1516). Oil painting, 32¼″ × 26⅜″. Louvre, Paris.

Blind Contour and Balance

away or off the sheet. The real or inferred line of an arm, the droop of a tree limb, the drape of cloth, or the direction of someone's gaze, all can keep the viewer's eye within the drawing or painting. Balance, and its effect on eye movement, is intrinsic to a good composition.

Balance, most times, infers stability since stable compositions can work for both symmetrical or asymmetrical approaches. Stable compositions are those that always appear firmly grounded, such as a pyramid or triangular structure (a portrait, arms folded across the waist, for instance). The broad base of a triangle provides the least propensity for falling over (see Figure 2.28).

A drawing that leads the eye up and up through the repetition of short horizontal roof tops to the perpendicular masses of the mountains behind, suggests a stable, vertical composition (see Figure 2.29).

FIGURE 2.29. Li Ch'eng (Ying-ch'iu) (active ca. 940–967, Chinese): *Buddhist Temple amid Clearing Mountain Peaks.* Ink and slight color on silk, 44″ × 22″. Nelson Gallery–Atkins Museum of Fine Arts.

FIGURE 2.30. George Caleb Bingham (1811–1879, American): *Fur Traders Descending the Missouri* (ca. 1845). Oil painting, 29″ × 36½″. Metropolitan Museum of Art, New York.

FIGURE 2.31. Peter Paul Rubens (1577–1640, Flemish): *The Small Final Judgment* (ca. 1620). Oil painting, 72³⁄₁₆″ × 46⅞″. Alte Pinakothek, Munich.

Blind Contour and Balance

A long, low canoe on quiet water, floating past an island in the foggy distance depicts a stable, horizontal composition (see **Figure** 2.30).

But balance may not always be stable. Unstable compositions can work for both symmetrical or asymmetrical approaches. Unstable compositions appear to be floating, or collapsing, or on the verge of either. Almost every unsupported diagonal, inverted pyramid, or spiral will look unstable (see Figure 2.31).

Each kind of composition—stable or unstable—is open to abuse or to beauty. Stable compositions can be soothing, uplifting, monotonous, or trite. Unstable compositions can lend marvelous tension to the meaning of a work; they can also take your eye right off the page in confusion.

Good composition is elusive, and the decisions required are numerous.

Composition is not so much identifiable as knowable, meaning that you can identify many aspects of a drawing and still not quite know why the composition is highly satisfactory or vaguely irritating. The fine art of knowing requires many studio experiences. Repeated analyses of works of art and a knowledge of art history help to build a more mature basis of reference from which to ask the question: What is good composition?

⌐ 3 ⌐

NEGATIVE CONTOUR

Tools
razor-tip black felt tip or a mechanical pen
smooth white drawing paper

Most persons, when they begin to draw, see objects as entities divorced from surrounding space. A bicycle, for instance, is drawn explicitly but floats in space. When drawing a still life composed of a bicycle, chair, and stool, a beginning student usually draws each object as a discrete part instead of seeing the still life shapes unified with surrounding shapes.

To move away from the object as object, try drawing "negative" shapes in a steady, solid contour line. A negative shape is defined as the shape of space that surrounds the object or that permeates it. The drawings opposite, a still life with bicycle, chain, and old stool, show both approaches—first the positive shapes (see Figure 3.1), then the same subject matter drawn with negative shapes (see Figure 3.2).

A series of negative shapes drawn from any subject matter will, when completed, *suggest* the positive shape of that which you are drawing. But the purpose of this exercise is to turn your thinking and seeing from the object itself, to that of seeing shapes of space which surround or permeate things. The process requires that you see space in a new way. Conventional spatial expectations are reoriented.

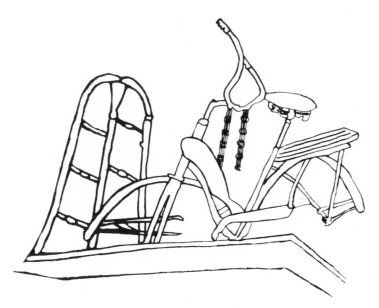

FIGURE 3.1. Still life showing positive shapes.

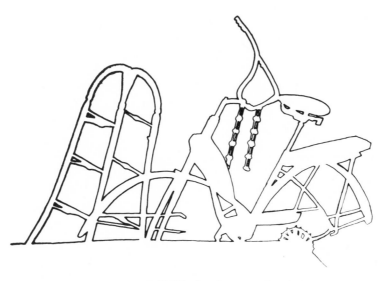

FIGURE 3.2. Still life showing negative shapes.

Some confusions are likely to arise: For example, when one line of the handle-bar section is completed and the second one is started, your drawing may look much like a positive shape, but your concern should remain on the negative space—in this case the space from the handle bars to the edge of the paper (see Figure 3.3). Let your eyes see *that* shape, not the positive one. Otherwise, you will still be isolating objects.

A second confusion occurs when a group of objects, positioned behind one another, forms one negative shape. The delineation of space in a negative-contour problem will suggest flatness. Objects lose their dimension because the problem requires that simultaneous negative shapes of overlapping objects in the still life be drawn irrespective of the illusion of depth. Drawing the negative shapes of each separate object misses the point of the exercise. Reducing depth is inherent in the problem: draw the negatives seen from your point of view, regardless of the separateness of the objects (see Figure 3.4).

A third confusion lies in "either/or" areas, which are sections of space that are not clearly positive or negative but which can be arbitrarily selected to help the composition. Such areas may be similar to the table top on which the bike is placed. An easy solution for the problem of stabilizing the composition (keeping the drawing from visually "floating" or sliding off) can be the use of a contour line to identify an edge that is either positive or negative (see Figure 3.2).

The viewer's perceptions should complete the drawing instinctively even though all visual data may not be drawn. An artist, even a beginner, need not state everything "realistically" to be understood.

Another brief word on composition: although composition is discussed throughout the book, at this stage it is best to select a specific *point of view,* such as the middle or the end of the still life. From your position, see whether the total composition is more nearly horizontal or vertical, then draw on the paper the way the composition most likely fits. Predominantly horizontal compositions look awkward when they are drawn on vertical paper because total use of space is not well conceived (see Figure 3.5).

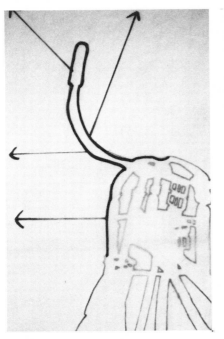

FIGURE 3.3. Negative shapes.

FIGURE 3.4. Negative shapes regardless of depth.

FIGURE 3.5. Horizontal composition on a vertical sheet.

FIGURE 3.6. Vertical composition on a horizontal sheet.

The same criteria apply to a vertical composition on a horizontal sheet (see Figure 3.6).

There is too much unused space in each of these examples. As a general rule, place a horizontal composition on a horizontal plane and a vertical composition on a vertical plane. Variations on rules is the main subject of the last chapter.

ANIMAL STUDIES
IN CONTOUR

TOOLS
2B and 3B pencils
white drawing paper
animal museum
drawing board

Dog Scratching Itself (see Figure 4.1) is a skillful drawing of a dog doing something all dogs do. The fact that the artist isolated this event and put us, the viewers, in the position he did (the point of view) prompts us to see the action as humorous.

An artist who has mastered drawing skills selects what will be shown and how the image will be presented. In *Dog Scratching Itself* the artist drew in contour line from a live animal, a difficult thing to do.

Our problem focuses on birds or animals that are mounted and hold still. If there is a natural-history museum near you, make use of it for this problem. If not, call a local science teacher, taxidermist, or a university biology or zoology department. Or find someone who has a mounted bird or animal.

Since most museum animals are confined in glass cases, access visually to the subject may be limited. Also, museums seldom provide chairs, so the floor is the most likely place to sit when you draw. Try to find a

FIGURE 4.1. Housebook Master: *Dog Scratching Itself* (ca. 1480–1490). Engraving. Rijksmuseum, Amsterdam.

bird or beast that appeals to you, then select your point of view, front, back, or side. Look at the whole shape of the animal. Will that animal's shape be interesting when it's drawn? If you think that point of view, the angle at which you are placed on the subject, is yielding a boring or uninteresting animal shape, move yourself to another position and reassess the possibilities. Or move on to a different animal.

Once you have found an animal and a position that will yield an interesting shape in translation, then look for background lines to use as part of the composition. The lines of the case, or the lines of the stand on which the animal is mounted will help "stabilize" your subject. Those same lines could also help identify the negative shapes surrounding your bird or animal.

In our culture, certain kinds of lines have fairly specific connotations. Vertical lines suggest a stabilized energy. Horizontal lines suggest a stabilized restfulness. Curvilinear lines suggest a pliant flow. Diagonals

Animal Studies in Contour

are dramatic and irritating. (That is the reason we have X signs at railroad crossings, to arrest the eye.)

If, in a drawing, an animal is placed in the middle of the paper, it will tend to look as though it is hanging in space and the composition will appear unresolved. If you choose an animal mounted on a diagonal limb, you are a prime candidate for drawing an oblique composition that will run the eye off the page (see Figure 4.2).

Find a different point of view, or stabilize the composition with some fairly defined verticals and horizontals taken from the edges of the case. Secure and orient the space in some way to keep the composition grounded.

Laying out a general composition on your paper with small half-inch lines could help (see Figure 4.3). Begin by looking at the highest point of your animal, and touch the paper with a pencil mark at the equivalent point. Do the same with the width of the animal, marking the half-inch lines at the equivalent widths on the paper. Do the same

FIGURE 4.2. Composition too low on the page.

FIGURE 4.3. Composition layout with ½-inch lines.

FIGURE 4.4. Student contour drawing of a mounted animal. Pencil on white drawing paper.

FIGURE 4.5. Animal form suggested with contour (tail).

with the bottom lines of the animal, remembering long tails if there are
any.

Many artists use a grid to help in seeing and translating proportional problems. Grids have long been used as an intermediate step
toward a finished piece of work. About arm's length, hold your pencil
vertically to the tip of the animal's ear. Note where on the vertical line
of your pencil something else touches the same edge of the pencil—an
eye, a foot, part of the chest. Lightly mark your paper with half-inch
lines at those proportions. Then hold your pencil horizontally. You may
notice that one ear is higher than the other, one eye lower. Perhaps the
edge of the duck's bill on the left comes just to the height of the tail
feathers. Put in only enough lightly drawn half-inch lines to guide you
in your drawing. You are establishing the general compositional layout.
Now you are ready to proceed to the core of the problem, the contour
drawing (see Figure 4.4).

Setting up the composition this way will help you realize the compositional unit afforded by the shape of your drawing paper. Preliminary layout helps with proportion and keeps your drawing from running off the page.

Two approaches with contour lines are possible here:

1. Draw a single contour line of the whole animal, constantly re-
viewing the vertical/horizontal measurements; or

2. Begin drawing the fur or feathers without the aid of an exterior contour line, leaving the animal form suggested (see Figure
4.5).

Up to this point, you have drawn fairly easy surfaces, such as metal,
wood, skin, or shoe leather. How does a student draw fur or feathers?
Obviously, you can't draw each feather or strand of fur, or quill of an
animal, but you can draw the *patterns* inherent in the topography of
the animal. From a frontal view of a fox, for example, the fur grows
up over the forehead, then comes down around the eyes into the cheeks
and jowels. *Look* at the fur and draw the lines in the patterns of the
"lay of the land." Be careful that you make those repetitive lines in-

FIGURE 4.6. Student contour drawing of a mounted animal. Pencil on white drawing paper.

FIGURE 4.7. Student contour drawing of a mounted duck. Pencil on white drawing paper.

Animal Studies in Contour

formative. It is very easy to become lax in observation and to stroke the paper meaninglessly over and over. Such lines quickly become uninteresting. *Look* at the fur, follow the patterns, but lay in the fur, quills, or tufts carefully.

It may be surprising to note that there are different qualities of fur on an animal. The porcupine is covered along the lower belly with soft fur, along the top back with very hard, sharp quills. So there have to be special characteristics in your lines to define those differences. Try pressing harder on your pencil whenever a more dramatic line is called for. Drawing a quill or a claw in one or two strong dark strokes says more about "quillness" and "clawness" than a tentative, light line.

Remember, we are not working in values (that is shading) in this problem. What, then, should you do about the variations of values in the animals and birds? Density of line is one solution. If the cheetah has dark spots, draw the lines closer together and press harder on the pencil. If the bird has white breast feathers, draw lightly. Feathers are cupped and overlayed, a difficult topography to draw. Do what you can, but resolving the translations of fur, feathers, scales, or skin may prove so discouraging that you feel seriously frustrated or defeated. Let such areas go until later, when you have had more experience and can find the visual solutions.

At this stage you are working for composition, for the structure of the animal, and for areas of the animal that best inform your contour lines (see Figures 4.6 and 4.7).

While the exercises in contour are set forth to help develop sensitivity with line, few artists in history employ just a single contour line. Usually, combinations of contour, gesture, or value are used, one sometimes more obvious than the others. In *Stag Hunt* (see Figure 4.8), the spare, clean linear rhythm predominates over the soft values of the men and animals.

FIGURE 4.8. Gnosis: *Stag Hunt* (ca. 300 B.C.). Floor mosaic. Pella Museum, Greece.

⌜ 5 ⌝

IMAGE INVERSION

Tools
2B pencil
white drawing paper
still life

Drawing a normal still life upside down may sound like a simple-minded exercise, but it stimulates the process of problem solving, partly because it requires active concentration. Inverting the still life requires thoughtful study so that you can invert whole shapes, both positive and negative. It will prompt you first to see what shapes are present in the still life and then to draw them upside down.

Your point of view should be broadside to the still life. After you have the knack of drawing straightforward subject matter upside down, try oblique angles, or dramatic perspectives.

Once again, look first for the shapes that will inform your composition, remembering that everything will be upside down, so the shapes you are translating are seen as inverted, like a reflection on water.

Try to work with this problem in much the same way as you worked with blind contour, making the compositional establishing lines first, then the vertical/horizontal proportional grid lines. Image inversion will demand an active observation of the still life. Keep the line steady. Visually, feel your way carefully and slowly over the contours and tex-

tures of the subject you are drawing. Just remember to draw it as upside down.

When you have finished the drawing, tack it on a wall, sit back, and
look at it. Try to see the unit of drawing simply as the breakup of
shapes and space. Forget you have drawn a bottle, blanket, wheel, or
copper kettle. Does the composition slide to one side? Is the composition small and planted in the middle of the page? Is the shape of the
large, external negative space surrounding the still life itself too large,
too small? Is the external, negative shape an interesting one?

Turn your drawing upside down now, making the image right side
up. Was accuracy a problem? If it was, you probably didn't put in
enough establishing lines before you started.

If some areas of the drawing seem awkward or boring, check the
still life again for more information in those areas. If you do not see
more interesting shapes than the ones with which you are dissatisfied,
you may indeed have reached a dead end with the drawing. Move yourself to an oblique position to the still life so that the new composition
will suggest more interesting shapes. Find the best information you can
in that still life. How you see what you see reflects your growing response to the drawing process (see Figure 5.1).

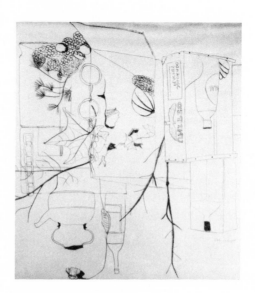

FIGURE 5.1. Inverted image.

⌐ 6 ⌐

CROSS CONTOUR

TOOLS
2B, 3B, and 4B pencils
white drawing paper
still life or model

Cross-contour drawing develops in much the same way as a scanner develops a parallel grid pattern for translating an image. An enlarged postage stamp, for instance, shows the use of variation of line to produce an image. With the aid of the thickness and thinness of the lines, the image emerges (see Figure 6.1).

This problem is similar to the tactile "blind contour" problem. But in cross contour you *feel* the whole space of the still life with your eyes —the in-and-out volume of the drapery, the solid structure of a ceramic or glass object, the cylindrical volume of bottle necks or chair legs. But the cross-contour problem does not take the object per se and follow only its contours. The cross-contour problem is meant to work with the entire space, positive and negative, top to bottom, left to right, line by line, each line scanning the still life's next quarter inch of space, vertically or horizontally.

To work through the problem you need to "feel" volume with your eyes and translate that feeling, line by parallel line, to a sheet of drawing paper.

However, this translation should make only limited use of value.

FIGURE 6.1. Engraved lines of a stamp showing cross-contour lines.

Show value simply in the pressure of the stroke, not by smearing and modulating values over large surfaces. Cross contour is a linear problem.

Find what you think is the most interesting position from which to approach your still life—below, above, to the side. Lay out the general composition on your paper with a few small half-inch indicator markings, drawn lightly. Look at the highest point of your composition, the lowest, the far left, and the far right. Then, as before, while using the vertical/horizontal measurements, lay in the most important establishing lines.

A student can approach this grid pattern several ways: top to bottom, left to right, right to left. Try to keep your lines close together. If they are too far apart, the final image won't "read" at all. A well-sharpened pencil and fairly close lines will work best.

Squinting helps identify lights and darks, so squint at the still life. Where are the highest lights and lowest darks? Those values are the extremes in your still life. The highest lights, obviously, will be indicated by the least pressure on the pencil, possibly so light that they are barely apparent on the drawing paper. The darkest darks will need the

Cross Contour

most pressure on the pencil and will thus be wider. In this problem, value contained only in the line gives the illusion of volume.

Find your starting point, which is usually at the top of your paper, working horizontally left to right or working vertically from the top down the paper.

As you draw the first line, vary the pressure according to the *volume* established, the topographical definition, by the light or lack of light— less pressure for more light, more pressure where the shadows are. Keep your eye moving with your pencil. Look carefully and proceed very slowly. This is a drawing task that cannot be hurried.

Occasionally a student will use the highest lights as a negative and not involve line at all in those spaces, but will break the line, then pick it up again when the value becomes dark enough (see Figure 6.2).

Such selectivity works as long as you keep the whole unit of space in

FIGURE 6.2. Student drawing of a still life in cross contour. Pencil on newsprint.

mind and not just objects in space. Following only the curvilinear surfaces of the individual still-life objects usually results in mere copying
of objects.

Even if you think you are on the wrong track, keep going. It's surprising to see that after five or six carefully drawn lines an image begins
to emerge (see Figures 6.3 and 6.4).

The power of the sensitive line rests in what it evokes from the
viewer. The length, the width, the pressured tones, all have connotations. The medium also will lend its own qualities to a line. Line can
be a beautiful and versatile form of expression, as you can see in two
very dissimilar cross-contour works. The anonymous German work, a
woodcut illustration from Virgil's *Aeneid* (see Figure 6.5), seems

FIGURE 6.3. Student drawing of
drapery in cross contour. Pencil
on white drawing paper.

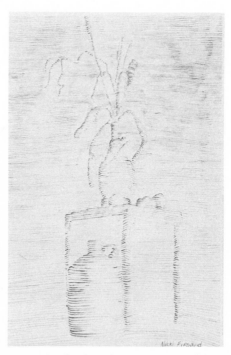

FIGURE 6.4. Student drawing of a still life
in cross contour. Pencil on white drawing
paper.

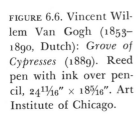

FIGURE 6.5. German: page from Virgil's *Aeneid* (1502). Woodcut, 12⅛″ × 8⅜″. Des Moines Art Center.

FIGURE 6.6. Vincent Willem Van Gogh (1853–1890, Dutch): *Grove of Cypresses* (1889). Reed pen with ink over pencil, 24¹¹⁄₁₆″ × 18⁵⁄₁₆″. Art Institute of Chicago.

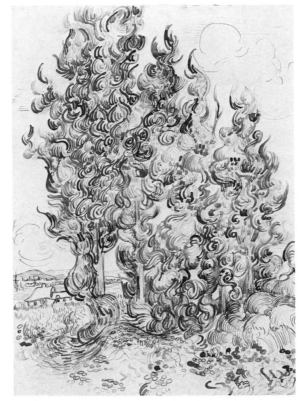

sculptural, like a bas-relief, effected by the very controlled thickness and thinness of lines. Van Gogh's curvilinear strokes in *Grove of Cypresses* (see Figure 6.6), drawn with reed pen and ink over pencil, suggests a motive energy in the otherwise stable trees.

⌐ 7 ⌐

DISTORTIONS

TOOLS
2B pencil
white drawing paper
concave or convex reflecting surface
  or convex transparent object

The distorted image was a major theme throughout the work of Parmigianino. From images derived from the use of curved mirrors, he developed a life-long obsession with distortion as subjective interpretation. Distortion is clearly seen in the early self-portrait painted from his reflection in a convex mirror (see Figure 7.1). During his brief career, Parmigianino developed a new breed of figures with elongated limbs and bodies not otherwise seen in nature.

A student sometimes wants to develop a similar breed, or distort for the sake of distortion. Imagination certainly has its place in art but a heavy reliance on imagination too early and too often can become a substitute for informed practice. Drawings look empty, stylized, and clichéd. At this stage, the richest possible information is taken from what you see. Drawing from space artificially distorted gives you a chance to translate from given atypical shapes. But those shapes, though distorted, retain intrinsic characteristics.

This problem of distortion is designed to apply contour drawing to ready-made distorted space, the sort of distortion produced by the re-

FIGURE 7.1. Francesco Mazzuoli, known as Parmigianino (1503–1540, Italian): *Self-Portrait* (1524). Panel, diameter 9⅝″. Kunsthistorisches Museum, Vienna.

fraction of a reflective surface such as a convex/concave mirror, chrome fender, hub cap, toaster, or polished steel spoon. A clear, curvilinear shape such as a glass, bottle, or camera lens will do as well.

Prop up the transparent, curved object or the curved reflective surface on or against something solid in order to stabilize it. Study the distortion. Determine what workable shapes are present. Experiment by moving the object around in order to find the most interesting composition. Your own reflected image can certainly be included.

If you are working with a reflective surface, be certain it has a high degree of reflection. Soft patinas will dull the shapes to be drawn. Drawing from the distorted space is difficult enough without struggling to see the reflection.

From the distorted image, use lines and shapes from objects in the room such as desks, chairs, lamps, and curtains to create your whole composition, perhaps incorporating your hand holding the glass or reflective object. Always remember to lay out the composition first, the

Distortions

perimeters and establishing lines. Draw carefully, draw slowly, working through the horizontal/vertical measurement, sighting with the pencil in order to keep the proportions as consistent as you can. Also, vary the pressure of your pencil to suggest what is concealed and to produce more expressive lines in the work.

Admittedly, the complexities of a curvilinear composition on a flat sheet are difficult, but unique to that rectangular space because most of the lines will be curved. Verticals and horizontals derived from objects in a room appear to bend. How do you stabilize a completely curved composition?

It would seem that since everything bends visually in a curved reflective or transparent image, the only inherent stability has to derive from one's memory, i.e., the desks, windows, walls, floors whose measure-

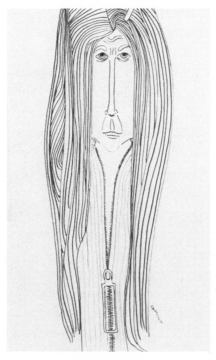

FIGURE 7.2. Student contour drawing of a distorted image. Pencil on newsprint.

FIGURE 7.3. Student contour drawing of a distorted image. Pencil on newsprint.

FIGURE 7.4. Student contour drawing of a distorted image. Pencil on white drawing paper.

ments are constant. A viewer knows pragmatically that the physical world is not distorted with bending objects, and such knowledge alone is a stabilizing factor. The composition of curvatures should, however, keep the eye moving within the composition. The contrapuntal balance of reciprocal lines and spaces tends to do just that. For instance, a single U shape can bring the eye into the composition and take it out again. A counterpoint line or shape to the U could be a reversed U shape overlapping the first one, ⊖ , so that the rhythm and movement of the drawing are self-contained and thus stabilized. Your total composition and the quality of your work will be better if you remember to work with counterforces of curved lines and shapes (see Figures 7.2, 7.3, and 7.4).

When Hans Holbein painted *Jean de Dinteville and Georges de Selves* (see Figure 7.5), distortion was treated in another way. The treatment is called anamorphosis, with the earliest drawing examples appearing in the notebooks of Leonardo da Vinci. An anamorphic image is distorted when viewed from a normal position. When a viewer adopts an oblique point of view, the image will appear correct. Holding Holbein's picture at eye level while turning the book to the left, as if on a vertical axis, the odd, unidentified streak should come into focus.

FIGURE 7.5. Hans Holbein the Younger (1493–1543, German): *Jean de Dinteville and Georges de Selves, or The Ambassadors* (1533). Oil and tempera on panel, 6′ 9½″ × 6′ 10½″. National Gallery, London.

⌈ 8 ⌉

LINEAR PERSPECTIVE

TOOLS
B pencil
white drawing paper
a cube, block, or box
3 sheets of tracing paper
ruler

Filippo Brunelleschi (1377–1446), the brilliant fifteenth-century Florentine architect and mathematician, constructed a device that identified and illustrated one of the most profound ideas of perspective: the
vanishing point. For his experiment, Brunelleschi stood just inside the
central doorway of the cathedral of Florence, his back to the square,
a piazza, in front of the cathedral. Placing a mirror on an easel before
him, he focused on the baptistery behind him. The reflection served as
the model for his small (one foot square) panel beside the mirror.[1]
With the precision of a miniature, he painted the scene. He represented
the sky with a burnished silver that could reflect the real sky and the
passing clouds. On completing his panel, Brunelleschi bored a hole
through it at precisely that point in the view which had been opposite
his eye when he painted it; that is, at the center of vision. The spectator was instructed to look through the hole from the back of the painting, and at the same time to hold a mirror on the far side in such a way
as to reflect the painting. "With the aforementioned elements of the

burnished silver, the piazza, the viewpoint," stated Antonio Manetti, Brunelleschi's biographer, "the spectator thought he saw the actual scene when he looked at the painting." [2]

Students often believe that what makes a drawing look "real" makes it "right." The multiplicity of visual systems—inverted perspective, parallel perspective, axial perspective, geometric or linear perspective, to name a few—testifies to the impossibility of arriving at any one entirely satisfactory "rightness" or "reality." An example of inverted perspective is seen in *The Last Judgment* (see Figure 8.1), which shows the point of convergence toward the eye rather than away from it.

However, the greatest part of Western art has conditioned our eyes and minds to feel that the most compelling characteristic of geometric or linear perspective is its vivid illusion of depth. And for that reason, this chapter concentrates on the principles of linear concerns.

The beginnings of the optical attitude, which we call Western perspective, are noticeable in the Greek red-figured vases, ca. 500 B.C. (see

FIGURE 8.1. *Last Judgment* (early eleventh century). Ottonian miniature from the *Book of Pericopes* of Henry II. Bayerische Staatsbibliothek, Munich.

FIGURE 8.2. The Foundry Painter: *Lapith and Centaur* (ca. 490–480 B.C.). Interior of an Attic red-figured kylix. Staatliche Antikensammlungen, Munich.

FIGURE 8.3. Inlay on a soundbox from a harp (ca. 2685 B.C.). From Ur, wood with inlaid gold, lapis lazuli, and shell. University Museum, Philadelphia.

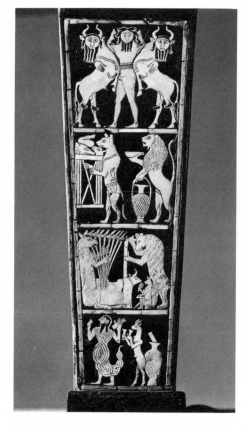

Figure 8.2). Experiments with foreshortening, a human foot in front view, for instance, were not seen in earlier works (see Figure 8.3) that showed forms in profile alone.

Perspective in Western drawing and painting developed from intuitive optical uses which later received a geometrical basis from principles laid down by Euclid in about 300 B.C. The thrust of Euclid's *Optics* was to express in mathematical language the precise relation between the actual quantities of objects and the apparent quantities that shape our visual image of them.

While Euclid's propositions were the cornerstone of the more developed geometric or Renaissance principles, not until the fifteenth century does *perspective* come to mean a method whereby the illusion obtained is from a fixed position while the artist looks through a transparent plane, draws the scene, and uses converging points (see Figure 8.4).

Binocular vision fuses visual information into one picture because each eyeball resembles a small camera. Images from the outside world are registered on a light-sensitive surface called the retina. As light rays pass through an opening known as the pupil, they behave as continuous straight lines until interrupted by the retinal screen. (Actually, behind the pupil at the lens, the top lines have intersected the bottom ones, so that the impression on the retina is inverted.) At no point on the retina is light accepted from more than a single point of an object. Therefore, any complete image is a composite of numerous line interruptions. Each object is joined to its image on the retina by a straight line.

That line, or light ray, which joins an object point to a retinal point is called, simply, a line of sight. The whole massive cluster of lines of sight available to the eyes is the cone of vision, its apex in the eyes and its base at the limits of what is seen (see Figure 8.5).

An imaginary, transparent plane parallel to the eyes (called the picture plane) placed anywhere between the object and the viewer is the plane on which the hypothetical image becomes the *perspective* of the original object. Thus, whenever a line of sight, a light ray, intersects the picture plane, a perspective point is denoted. That point will stand

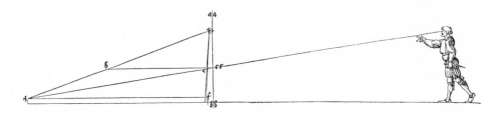

FIGURE 8.4. Albrecht Dürer (1471–1528, German): illustration from *Underweisung der Messung mit dem Birkel und Richtscheit* (1525). Woodcut.

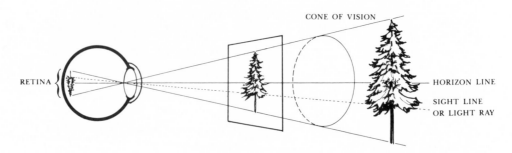

FIGURE 8.5. The eye, the inverted image on the retina, the light rays or sight lines, and the cone of vision.

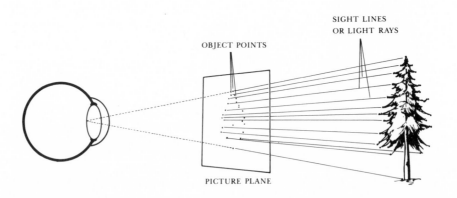

FIGURE 8.6. Sight lines or light rays intersecting the picture plane become the image of the object seen in perspective.

Linear Perspective

FIGURE 8.7. Albrecht Dürer (1471–1528, German): *Draftsman Drawing a Lute* (1525). Woodcut, 5³⁄₁₆″ × 7³⁄₁₆″.

for any point position along the sight line between the original object point and the picture plane (see Figures 8.6 and 8.7).

The eye (actually, the brain) is deceived into thinking it sees the original object point, whereas it sees the illusion, perspective (see Figure 8.8).

Because a drawing or painting is geometrically correct does not mean it is beautiful or even very good. Perspective, or the illusion of depth, was shelved or transformed into other modes for the better part of a thousand years, as seen in works from the early Christian, Byzantine, Carolingian, Ottonian, Romanesque, and early Gothic periods. The flat, the schematic, the symbolic, the hieratic (sacred), all have components that move a viewer. Placed in history these works of art display a spatial naïveté in order that other concerns become more important, such as narrative clarity, as in Biblical illustrations for the illiterate. And, for reasons other than geometric correctness, the works become

FIGURE 8.8. Albrecht Dürer (1471–1528, German): *Draftsman Drawing a Portrait* (1525). Woodcut, 5³⁄₁₆″ × 5⁷⁄₈″.

FIGURE 8.9. Simone Martini (ca. 1284–1344, Sienese): *Annunciation* (1333). Panel, 104⅛″ × 120⅛″. Uffizi Gallery, Florence.

art and move a viewer. Consider two examples: Simone Martini's *Annunciation*, 1333 (see Figure 8.9), and a portion of the Deësis mosaic, *Byzantine Christ* (see Figure 8.10).

For the angel, Martini portrays a billowing cloak, suggesting a posture of immediate arrival, knees first. Mary's turning away seems to acknowledge immediacy and surprise. Sacred symbolism and gold space notwithstanding, Martini captures a humanized event.

The Deësis mosaic, constructed with small gold tesserae, also achieves an atypical space, but the work aims to intensify the spiritual nature of Christ. The floating figure, the frontality, the benevolent stare, suggest otherwordliness.

On the other hand, Masaccio's use of linear perspective is the denominator for the surprising power of his painting. Masaccio is credited with the earliest painting using linear-perspective principles with a convergence point (see Figure 8.11).

Linear perspective is a tool, and you should be able to use it to your advantage. However, preoccupation with linear perspective restricts artistic freedom and can cause a drawing to become dry and mechanical like a rendering. But the principles are very useful to understand

FIGURE 8.10. *Byzantine Christ* (ca. thirteenth century). Detail of the Deësis mosaic, Hagia Sophia, Istanbul.

FIGURE 8.11. Tommaso Guidi, known as Masaccio (1401–1428, Italian): *Trinity* (1425).
Fresco, 21′ 10½″ × 10′ 5″. Santa Maria Novella, Florence.

and apply, with accuracy or educated distortion, toward creative ends so that a spatial authority is evident in your work. A word to the wise: use the illustrations hereafter provided as occasions to practice the processes described.

Perspective is defined as the representation on a plane of the spatial relation of objects as they might appear to the eye. Perspective deals with what you see from a specific point of view (looking up, down, or straight ahead) at a specific place, your station point. Perspective deals with the appearance of reality. Holding a dinner plate before you, flat side parallel to your eyes, the plate is geometrically a circle, its real shape. Standing in the same place, but with the plate slanted in a dish rack, you see the *appearance* of a circle, an ellipse.

Illusory depth, perspective, can be achieved several ways:

A. *Linear perspective:* the appearance of depth through receding line.

  Principles:
  1. Diminution—the decreasing of scale (see Figure 8.12).
  2. Foreshortening—the shortening proportionately of size by the revolving of the shape (see Figure 8.12).
  3. Convergence—the coming together of apparently parallel lines (see Figure 8.12).

B. *Aerial perspective:* The appearance of depth through atmospheric effects.

  Principle:
  1. The definition of objects is diminished by distance (see Figure 2.25).
      a. Forms blur and become less distinct.
      b. Values and colors lose their intensity.
      c. Textures become less evident.

C. *Overlap:* Depth is achieved in drawings when lines or volumes are placed in front of or behind others (see Figure 9.8).

D. *Light source and cast shadows:* Forms obstructing light imply depth.

Principles:

1. Vertical lines cast shadows in the direction of the light rays, on a plane (see Figure 8.34).
2. A line parallel to a plane casts a shadow parallel to itself (see Figures 8.39 and 8.40).

Overlapping planes and volumes in a foreshortening problem will be discussed in the next chapter. Principles of *aerial perspective* are applied mainly in drawing or painting far distances and will not be explored here. The student might profit from studying some of Joseph Mallord William Turner's later works from the 1830s and 1840s, or Camille Corot's work from the 1820s and 1830s to see uses of atmospheric conditions based on the principles of aerial perspective.

The principles of *linear perspective* are the main thrust of this chapter. Inevitably, an illustrated glossary of terms is a first priority.

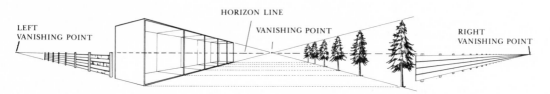

FIGURE 8.12. Diminution, foreshortening, convergence.

THE HORIZON LINE

The horizon line is a line always horizontal at your eye level wherever you are: on a mountain, in a building, lying on the ground (see Figures 8.13 a, b, c). Whether you look up, down, or straight ahead, the horizon line remains at your eye level (see Figures 8.13 d, e, f). Visible or not, the horizon line should be established in your drawings, even if in extreme cases the line is off the sheet of paper. Whether on or off the paper, its position will denote whether you are looking up (a low placement), down (a high placement), or straight ahead (in the middle). (See Figures 8.13 g, h, i).

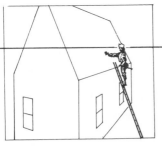

FIGURE 8.13a. Horizon line, high.

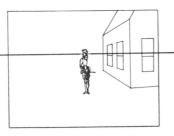

FIGURE 8.13b. Horizon line, middle.

FIGURE 8.13c. Horizon line, low.

FIGURE 8.13d. Andrea Mantegna (1431–1506, Italian): *St. James Led to His Execution* (ca. 1455). Pen drawing, 6⅛″ × 9¼″. British Museum, London.

FIGURE 8.13e. Winslow Homer (1836–1910, American): *The Morning Bell* (ca. 1866). Oil on canvas, 24″ × 38¼″. Yale University Art Gallery, New Haven.

FIGURE 8.13f. Albrecht Altdorfer (ca. 1485–1538, German): *Battle of Alexander* (1529). Lime panel, 62¼″ × 47¼″. Alte Pinakothek, Munich.

FIGURE 8.13g. Hilaire Germain Edgar Degas (1834–1917, French): *Estelle Musson* (ca. 1872). Pastel, 25″ × 22⅞″. Metropolitan Museum of Art, New York.

FIGURE 8.13h. Maurice-Quentin de La Tour (1704–1788, French): *Portrait of Jean-Marc Nattier* (ca. 1760). Pastel, 13¼″ × 10⅞″. Musée de Picardie, Amiens.

FIGURE 8.13i. Hilaire Germain Edgar Degas (1834–1917, French): *Portrait of Mademoiselle Lisle* (ca. 1869). Pastel and red crayon on buff paper, 8⅝″ × 10⅛″. Metropolitan Museum of Art, New York.

THE CONE OF VISION

Your position and your point of view (looking up, down, ahead) need to remain relatively fixed in order to draw with linear perspective. Your "field of vision" extends from your eyes like a cone radiating any number of sight lines to places where the eye rests. Those sight lines actually are light rays, bouncing from points off the subject, funneled to the eye.

The angle of the cone is approximately 30 degrees to 60 degrees, top to bottom, left to right. The cone of vision helps establish the boundaries of the picture you draw (see Figure 8.14).

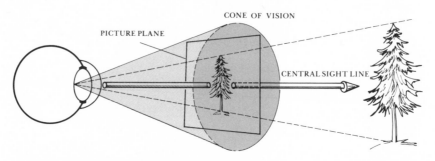

FIGURE 8.14. The cone of vision within which the picture plane is placed on which the perspective image is viewed.

THE CENTRAL SIGHT LINE

The central sight line is the line of most concentrated vision in the center of the cone (see Figure 8.14).

THE PICTURE PLANE

The picture plane is an imaginary plane of clear glass at a constant right angle to the central sight line, and, in other words, always parallel to your eyes. The picture plane becomes equivalent to the surface on which you draw. You must look one way for your visual information, look another way to transpose that information to the paper on which you draw, thereby making your drawing paper synonymous with the picture plane.

The picture plane, with its constant right angle to the central sight lines (see Figure 8.14), can be placed close to or far from your eye. But to draw without distortion, your distance from the picture plane and its distance from the subject have to be far enough away to encompass the height and width of the subject. Whether you are drawing a still life, a figure, a landscape, a large building, or a selected portion of a subject, this principle holds true.

THE STATION POINT

The station point is your position for drawing. The station point has to be established in two ways:

1. by the *lateral relationship* to the object (left, middle, right, oblique, or parallel);

2. by the *distance from* the object.

VANISHING POINTS

The illusion of depth hangs on the principle of convergence: lines that are parallel in actual sight will, if uninterrupted, meet at some point in infinity. This convergence is most notable in the conduct of lines that follow the direction of our central sight line and remain horizontal to the ground. As these lines seem to move away from us, the space that separates them diminishes until, at their meeting, diminution is complete. That point of convergence, in infinity, is represented by a vanishing point. For horizontal lines, such points will always be located on the horizon line (see Figure 8.15). Parallel lines of an object above the horizon line will converge downward. Parallel lines of an object below the horizon line will converge upward. Horizontal lines parallel to the picture plane do not converge. Vertical lines parallel to the picture plane do not converge unless you draw looking up or down, thereby tilting the angle of the picture plane (see Figure 8.15). Then parallel vertical lines will converge to a vertical vanishing point on a common infinity line perpendicular to the ground.

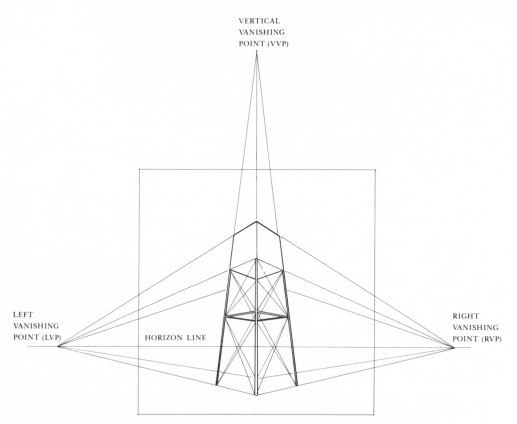

VERTICAL
VANISHING
POINT (VVP)

LEFT
VANISHING
POINT (LVP)

RIGHT
VANISHING
POINT (RVP)

HORIZON LINE

FIGURE 8.15. Families of receding parallel lines converge to separate vanishing points, each of which is beyond the boundary of the picture plane.

The phrase "receding parallel lines" is a shorthand reference to the illusion created by any set of lines that converge at the same point.

You will notice in Figure 8.15, that all the vanishing points are beyond the immediate boundaries of the picture plane, yet each vanishing point has been established. To place vanishing points that rest outside the picture plane, simply extend the horizon line or the vertical infinity line to such a distance that the vanishing points can be placed. A method for doing this is described on the following pages.

A serviceable example for explaining horizon lines and vanishing points is a checkered floor (see Figure 8.16). Euclid's fourth proposition serves well here: "Those things seen within a larger angle appear larger and those things seen within a smaller angle appear smaller."

Standing in the middle of the floor, the lines of sight pointing to the sides in the foreground make steeper and wider angles than those

Linear Perspective

pointing farther away. As the angles of sight decrease and become narrower with distance, the sight lines become more horizontal to the ground until at infinity the sight lines are virtually parallel to the floor, diminution is complete, and the convergence point is directly opposite your eye. That point in infinity is represented by a vanishing point on the horizon line of the picture plane.

Because all receding lines parallel to the ground converge on the horizon line (always at your eye level), finding the vanishing point is done simply by letting your eyes, aided by a pointing forefinger, if necessary, continue to trace the perceived lines to the horizon line. When that pointing line touches the horizon line of the picture plane, the vanishing point is established. If the vanishing point is beyond the perimeters of the picture plane, extend the horizon line far enough so that the pointing action can position the vanishing point. Actually, the principle of convergence holds true for any set of receding parallel lines.

If the lines are parallel and vertical to the ground, they will appear to converge to a vertical vanishing point, above you looking up, below you

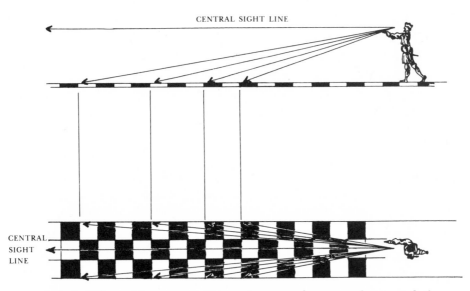

FIGURE 8.16. "Those things seen within a larger angle appear larger and those things seen within a smaller angle appear smaller."

looking down, on a line perpendicular to the ground called a vertical infinity line (see Figure 8.17).

For our purposes, placing the vertical infinity line can be done the following way. From your station point, while looking up at a building (the picture plane now tilted but remaining at right angles to the central sight line), point with your eyes or forefinger in the same direction the verticals recede. When the pointing line touches the picture plane, that point becomes the vertical vanishing point from which a line can be drawn perpendicular to the base line of the picture plane, establish-

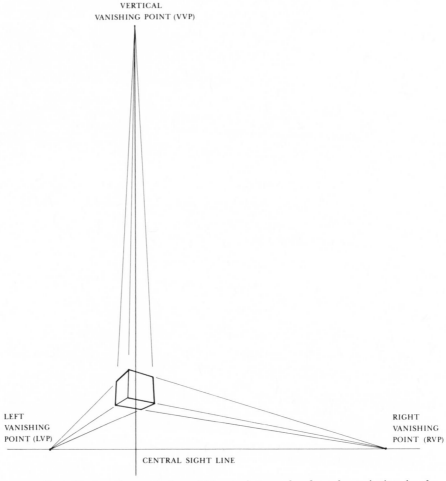

FIGURE 8.17. Placing the vertical vanishing point can be done by pointing in the same direction the parallel vertical lines recede.

ing the vertical infinity line. Extend the vertical infinity line beyond the picture plane if necessary, in order to place a vertical vanishing point.

Inclined planes—a slanted roof, for instance—present a variation of positioning the vertical infinity line and vertical vanishing points, but are kept within the system of three points. The idiosyncrasies of inclined planes are too numerous for full discussion here.

THE CUBE

To help clarify horizon lines and vanishing points more thoroughly, obtain a cube and use it as a model to help visualize the descriptions below. Any cube shape will do, a child's block, a plexiglass box, a square canister, etc.

Place the cube at eye level (see Figure 8.18), looking directly at one vertical corner (aligned with your central sight line) creating equal angles at the picture plane. If you point with your eyes or forefinger in the same direction as the receding horizontal cube edges, two vanishing points are established on the horizon line, one right and one left.

1. *Two-point perspective* is a term used when objects are oblique to the picture plane, the verticals remain parallel to the picture plane, and the receding horizontal parallels converge to a left and right vanishing point, necessitating two vanishing points. For two-point perspective, any number of objects oblique to the picture plane can be drawn, with each object establishing its own *pair* of vanishing points on the horizon line.

2. Since the vertical corner edge of the cube is aligned with the central sight line, forming equal angles to the picture plane, the left vanishing point and the right vanishing point are equidistant from the cube, the closest position they can occupy to each other.

Foreshorten the cube by turning it to your right (see Figure 8.19).

1. The vertical corner edge of the cube will not align with the central line of sight, creating unequal angles at the picture plane.

2. The left vanishing point is farther away from the corner of the cube than the right vanishing point.

Turn the cube far enough to the right so that what was the left side of the cube is now parallel to your picture plane (see Figure 8.20).

1. Now, a new set of receding parallel lines aligns with the right-side parallels, and all converge to one point, opposite the eye, creating a one-point perspective. What was the left side of the cube, now brought parallel to the picture plane, contains horizontals parallel to the picture plane, making the right vanishing point and left vanishing point an infinite distance apart.

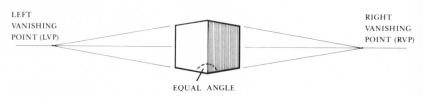

FIGURE 8.18. The cube at eye level with one corner aligned with your central sight line.

FIGURE 8.19. By turning the cube to the right, the left vanishing point moves farther from the corner than the right vanishing point. The central sight line does not remain aligned with the corner.

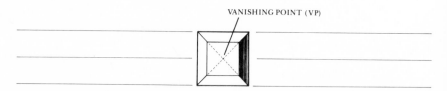

FIGURE 8.20. Now the former right vanishing point and the left vanishing point are an infinite distance apart, and a new single vanishing point is established.

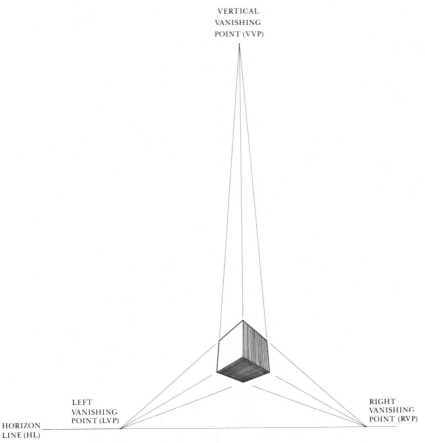

LEFT
VANISHING
POINT (LVP)

RIGHT
VANISHING
POINT (RVP)

HORIZON
LINE (HL)

FIGURE 8.21. A three-point perspective cube has no side parallel to the picture plane, and three groups of parallels converge to three separate vanishing points.

Place the cube above you, high enough so that you must look up to it (see Figure 8.21).

1. Any rectangular object drawn in this position will have horizontal parallels receding to a left vanishing point and right vanishing point on the horizon line with verticals receding to a vertical vanishing point on a vertical infinity line. *Three-point perspective* is a term used when an object has no side parallel to the picture plane so that three groups of parallels, the verticals and two sets of horizontals, converge to three separate vanishing points.

2. The problem described demonstrates three-point perspective when the station point is near the ground and the resulting vertical

convergence is *up*. Convergence *down* occurs when the station point is near the top of a building, a mountain, etc., and the viewer looks down.

The true one-point perspective has the vanishing point in the middle of the cone of vision on the horizon line. Technically speaking, if a room and its contents are parallel to your picture plane (the vanishing point is in the middle of the room on the horizon line), and you move to the right or left while looking at the same place, or if you look a little to the right or left while in one position, you have subtly changed your point of view to a two-point perspective. The picture plane is no longer parallel but slightly oblique to the room and its contents. And if you climb on a chair or stoop down while looking at the same place, you have moved into a three-point perspective with vertical vanishing points.

Technical limits are stretched sometimes to create distortions or to avoid them, but you should be aware of what you are doing.

The principle systems for deriving linear perspective discussed in this book originated in the fifteenth century with Brunelleschi and his friend Alberti. Brunelleschi is generally credited as the creator of an architectural system that included a plan drawing, the elevation view, and intersection points on a picture plane. That method is still used in architecture. Some fifteen years later, Alberti devised a process he thought more suitable "for artists." He used a checkered floor, and demonstrated on a picture plane that the lines of the floor appear to recede to a "centric" point. Further, the picture plane could be used as a grid to measure heights in receding depth.

A presentation of certain aspects of the two systems, somewhat condensed in format, is included in Chapter Thirty-one. Called the office or common method, the procedures detail more exact ways for achieving one-, two-, and three-point perspective drawings.

EXERCISES

1. Below are photographs that utilize one-, two-, and three-point perspective (see Figures 8.22, 8.23, and 8.24). Using a separate

FIGURE 8.22. Using a sheet of tracing paper, trace the receding parallel lines to the vanishing point on this one-point perspective of a house interior.

FIGURE 8.23. Using a sheet of tracing paper, trace the receding parallel lines to their vanishing points on this two-point perspective of Timberlake Playhouse.

FIGURE 8.24. Using a sheet of tracing paper, trace the receding parallel lines to their vanishing points on this three-point perspective of the Shimer bell-tower.

sheet of tracing paper over each, trace the receding parallel lines to their vanishing points. Once the vanishing points are positioned, you can identify the horizon line and/or the vertical infinity line.

2. Practice drawing a box or your cube from different angles to the picture plane while it is

    a. even with your eye level;
    b. somewhat above your eye level;
    c. placed by your feet.

Remember to

• station yourself far enough away so that your cone of vision and picture plane encompass the height and width of the box;

• check your central sight line, which will be the center of your drawing;

• lightly draw the horizon line on or off the paper, as the case may be;

• estimate the height of the box corner closest to you, draw it, then place the vanishing points.

3. Two-point perpspective is most commonly used. Try a freehand drawing of a building in a landscape. Again, station yourself far enough away so that your cone of vision and picture plane encompass the height and width of whatever you want to draw. Remember, the building, to be two-point perspective, has to be oblique to your picture plane. Check your central sight line, which will be the center of your drawing. Lightly draw the horizon line. Establish the height of the building corner closest to you, then place the vanishing points. Lay in the receding parallel lines of doors, windows, trees, sidewalks, etc. Once the linear perspective is lightly "laid in," finish the drawing in contour line, remembering *now* that your line is to be sensitive in translating the forms you draw, not mechanical (see Figure 8.25).

FIGURE 8.25. A building drawn in contour line.

EQUAL UNITS IN DEPTH

A general principle to follow is this: *the diagonals of any square or rectangle will always intersect at the exact center.* This principle holds true whether you view a true square or a square in perspective. In a true square or rectangle the diagonals meet at a point equidistant from top and bottom. In perspective the diagonals will meet at a point closer to the top or bottom, but the center will be accurately placed where the diagonals cross.

Using squares or rectangles receding in space placed at equal distances is relatively easy, if one views them as fence posts.

The basic information needed is the horizon line, the vanishing point, the placement of the first two posts (which sets the distance between the rest of the posts as they recede), and diagonals between the two to identify the center of the posts (see Figure 8.26).

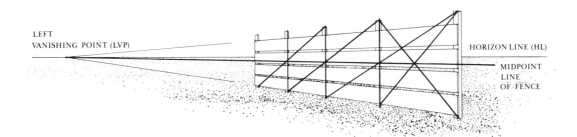

LEFT
VANISHING POINT (LVP)

HORIZON LINE (HL)

MIDPOINT
LINE
OF FENCE

FIGURE 8.26. The diagonals of any square or rectangle will always intersect at the exact center, whether the square or rectangle is true or in perspective.

1. Establish the horizon line and vanishing point.

2. In the foreground, draw two posts—that is, two vertical lines.

3. From the tops and bottoms of the posts draw the receding parallel lines to the vanishing point.

4. From the top of each post to the bottom of the other (the square or rectangle in perspective), draw a diagonal line, and the midpoint for the fence is identified.

5. Through that midpoint, draw a line to the vanishing point.

6. Placing the third post is done simply by drawing a diagonal from the top of post 1 through the middle of post 2. The point where that diagonal line intersects the receding ground line of the fence positions post 3. Draw the vertical post and continue the same process as far "back" as you need to draw the fence.

CIRCLES AND CENTERS IN PERSPECTIVE

Finding the centers of circles is necessary to drawing because centers very often are the gravitational lines or balance lines of something that, drawn off-center, appears inclined or falling over.

But finding centers is a process complicated by paradox: one must see the circle simultaneously *in perspective*—that is, as a foreshortened shape in space—and *vertically*—that is, as an ellipse standing on its edge. The centers for each of the shapes are derived from placing straight-line enclosures around the perimeters and then locating common intersections. Both views of the circle must be kept in mind.

The center of a true circle encased by a true square is found at the intersection of the diagonals of the square (see Figure 8.27). The center of a circle in perspective is found the same way (see Figure 8.27). The square is drawn first in perspective, then the circle within that square. With the diagonals of that square in perspective (a trapezoid), you can locate the center of the foreshortened circle, though the top and bottom sections are unequal.

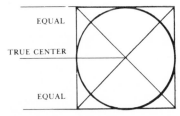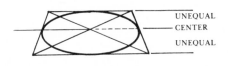

FIGURE 8.27. The center of a circle encased by a square is found at the intersection of the diagonals of the square, whether true or in perspective.

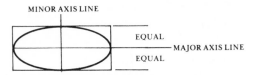

FIGURE 8.28. The ellipse (circle in perspective), encased in a rectangle and divided into four equal sections, forms axis lines.

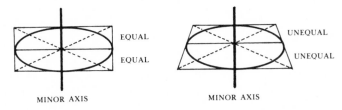

FIGURE 8.29. The pivotal line for a circle in perspective is the minor axis of the ellipse.

A circle in perspective has an elliptical shape. The ellipse must now be encased in a rectangle. The vertical and horizontal midpoint dividing lines of the rectangle, called axis lines, are at right angles and form four equal quadrants (sections) of the ellipse (see Figure 8.28).

But an axis belongs to something that revolves, meaning a body in space, and here is the paradox. The pivotal line for a *circle in perspective* is the minor axis of the *ellipse,* on edge (see Figure 8.29).

The major axis of an ellipse divides its longest or widest dimension. The minor axis divides its shortest dimension. An ellipse, at any angle to the picture plane, always has its major and minor axes at right angles.

When drawing circles in perspective as if they were objects like tires, cylinders, lampshades, etc., extend the minor axis of the ellipse through the center point of the circle in perspective (encased in the trapezoid) so that the minor axis line becomes the center line of what is being drawn—i.e., the wheel's axle, the bar of the barbells, etc. (see Figure 8.30).

LIGHT RAYS AND CAST SHADOWS

Historically, several types of lighting have been used in drawings and paintings. "Holy light" was employed in scenes illustrating religious subjects as seen in Gentile da Fabriano's *Nativity* (see Figure 8.31). Isolated figures glow internally with a phosphorescence, radiating strange and inconsistent shadows.

In *Ambroise Vollard,* a cubist painting by Picasso (see Figure 8.32), you can see how general illumination plays over a field of interest where shadows do not exist. Shading does, but not cast shadows.

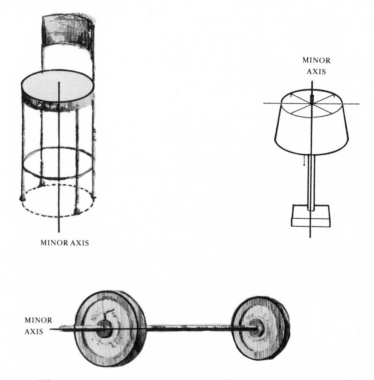

FIGURE 8.30. The minor axis becomes the center line of the lamp stand and the bar of the barbells.

FIGURE 8.31. Francesco di Gentile da Fabriano (ca. 1370–1427, Italian): *Nativity,* from *Adoration of the Magi* predella (1421). Panel, 12¼″ × 29¼″. Uffizi Gallery, Florence.

FIGURE 8.32. Pablo Picasso (1881–1973, Spanish): *Ambroise Vollard* (1909–1910). Oil on canvas, 36″ × 26½″. Pushkin Museum, Moscow.

FIGURE 8.33. Georges de La Tour (1593–1652, French): *St. Joseph the Carpenter* (ca. 1645). Oil on canvas, 38½″ × 25″. Louvre, Paris.

Since a light source close to the subject, such as a light bulb or candle, radiates light rays, the cast shadows also will be radial. Georges de La Tour painted a number of works that used candles as a light source (see Figure 8.33).

The sun, because it is so far away, is viewed as casting parallel rays. The sun's position prescribes the angle at which the rays are cast; vertical edges then cast shadows in the same direction. *The Morning Bell* by Winslow Homer (see Figure 8.34) suggests this kind of cast shadow.

In drawing shadows there are two principles to keep in mind:

1. vertical lines will cast shadows in the direction of the light rays on a plane;

2. a line parallel to a plane casts a shadow parallel to itself.

Shadows that read well in a drawing are cast in the right direction and have a specific length. The length of a cast shadow depends on the

FIGURE 8.34. Winslow Homer (1836–1910, American): *The Morning Bell* (ca. 1866). Oil on canvas, 24″ × 38¼″. Yale University Art Gallery, New Haven.

angle of the light rays. All angles are possible. The shadow's length is determined when the light ray, in a straight line, passes the topmost point of an object and meets the plane on which the object rests (see Figure 8.35).

A strictly parallel view, like the example, is never possible, because a shadow, to be perceived, must be either above or below a horizon line. How, then, do you know the angle of a light ray? Navigators and engineers have tools for determining light angles, but you will need to estimate. First, place the height of the object, then position the light source. Cast shadows are then drawn in a consistent relationship with the angle denoted by the first two placements.

If objects are lit with a candle, principle number 1 applies. The direction and length of a candle-cast shadow are obtained by drawing a line from the flame of the candle to pass through the top of the shapes lit. The direction of the shadows will radiate along lines from the base of the candle, but will themselves extend from the base of the object to converge with the light ray at the first unobstructed point (see Figure 8.36).

If the light source is a bulb above a table, again the same principle

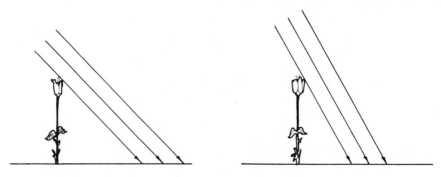

FIGURE 8.35. The length of a cast shadow depends on the angle of the light rays.

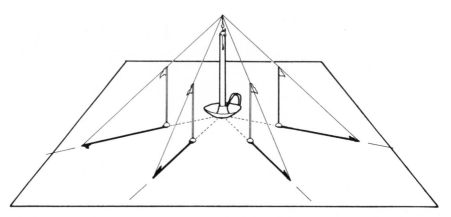

FIGURE 8.36. Vertical lines will cast shadows in the direction of the light rays, on a plane. In this case a candle was used, and the shadows radiate from the light source.

applies. From the bulb, drop a line to a point on the table directly below the light source. Draw a line from the light source through the top of the shapes lit. The shadow's direction will radiate from the dropped point on the table, but extend from the base of the object to the light ray that converges at the first unobstructed point (see Figure 8.37).

When the sun's rays are not parallel to the picture plane (for instance, if the sun is in front of you so that the object is back-lit), ray lines must appear to converge at the light source. There will now be three sets of convergence points: the light source itself (denoted by a small circle), the shadow's vanishing point (on the horizon line directly below the sun), and the general vanishing points of the object itself, also located on the horizon line (see Figure 8.38).

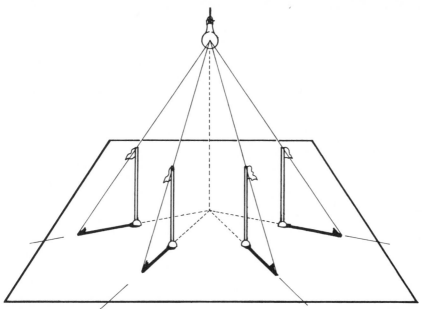

FIGURE 8.37. Again, vertical lines will cast shadows in the direction of the light rays, on a plane. In this case a light bulb was used, and the shadows radiate from the light source.

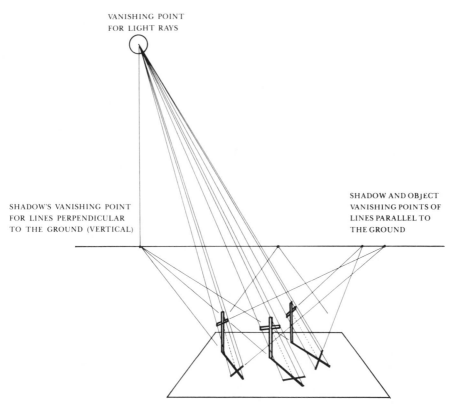

VANISHING POINT
FOR LIGHT RAYS

SHADOW'S VANISHING POINT
FOR LINES PERPENDICULAR
TO THE GROUND (VERTICAL)

SHADOW AND OBJECT
VANISHING POINTS OF
LINES PARALLEL TO
THE GROUND

FIGURE 8.38. When the sun's rays are not parallel to the picture plane, there will be three sets of convergence points.

Establish the horizion line, place the sun, and drop a line vertically from the sun to the horizon line. The intersection becomes the shadow's vanishing point. Locate the object's vanishing points by finding where its receding parallel lines meet the horizon. So much for shadows cast by vertical lines.

A line parallel to a plane casts a shadow parallel to itself. Principle number 2 is consistent with any of the light sources heretofore discussed (see Figure 8.39).

Because the top line of the object is parallel to the plane on which it rests (table top), it follows that to complete the shape of the cast shadow, drawing another line to the object's vanishing point is the solution.

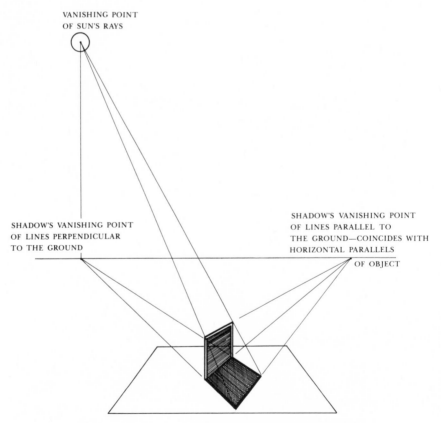

VANISHING POINT
OF SUN'S RAYS

SHADOW'S VANISHING POINT
OF LINES PERPENDICULAR
TO THE GROUND

SHADOW'S VANISHING POINT
OF LINES PARALLEL TO
THE GROUND—COINCIDES WITH
HORIZONTAL PARALLELS
OF OBJECT

FIGURE 8.39. A line parallel to a plane casts a shadow parallel to itself.

Linear Perspective

Drawing cubes will create another set of cast shadow points, but the two major principles still apply (see Figure 8.40).

This chapter is not the place to prolong discussion and multiply exercises with perspective problems. They are numerous, and if you wish to work with them, you will profit by studying from books on perspective found in a library.

Stretching beyond the fundamental perspective concerns examined in this chapter is a large and interesting assortment of them. Included are linear perspective distortion problems, elongated heights and widths in perspective, and unequal space sequences in depth. There are problems in drawing circular staircases, archways, columns, domes, views uphill and downhill, cones, and complex shadows. Information

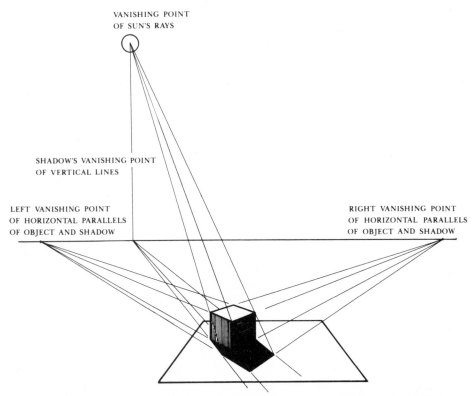

FIGURE 8.40. Remember, vertical lines cast shadows in the direction of the light rays, on a plane, and a line parallel to a plane casts a shadow parallel to itself.

FIGURE 8.41. Pietro Berrettini, known as Pietro da Cortona (1596–1669, Italian): *Glorification of the Reign of Urban VIII* (1633–1639). Detail of ceiling fresco, Palazzo Barberini, Rome.

can be found on drawing mirror perspective, reflections, and anamorphic images (of which the underlying principle is negative perspective, or the adjustment of proportions to counteract the normal "perspective" as in looking at a statue overhead).

A student of art during the Renaissance or Baroque periods would probably have been compelled to try every approach possible for drawing an illusion. Do not hesitate to be any less venturesome.

9

FORESHORTENING
IN CONTOUR

TOOLS
2B and 3B pencils
white drawing paper
model
drawing board

While looking at a drawing or a painting, a viewer's degree of responsiveness is not a direct correlate to the scale of the work. A reaction of heightened intensity can be induced even though images may be, literally, only several inches high. Scale and point of view may serve to move a viewer.

Comparing Mantegna's small drawing and his subsequent fresco of *St. James Led to His Execution* (see Figures 9.1 and 9.2), one can see that the point of view in the fresco (the vanishing point on the horizon line is below the picture, causing us to look up) intensifies our feelings of the miracle performed by Saint James, who, on the way to his own execution stops to bless and heal a paralytic. Some viewers may feel the fresco is too dramatic and the small drawing is the more meaningful though less flamboyant. The principal contrast is not simply one of scale, but of point of view. The fresco is the final version of the preliminary drawing. Mantegna purposely and skillfully placed us where he did to unify the form and content of his work.

FIGURE 9.1. Andrea Mantegna (1431–1506, Italian): *St. James Led to His Execution* (ca. 1455). Pen drawing, 6⅛″ × 9¼″. British Museum, London.

FIGURE 9.2. Andrea Mantegna (1431–1506, Italian): *St. James Led to His Execution* (ca. 1455). Fresco. Ovetari Chapel, Church of Eremitani, Padua.

There is a well-known poster by James Montgomery Flagg of Uncle Sam pointing a finger at the observer commanding, "I want you" (see Figure 9.3). The illusion that poster presents is that Uncle Sam's arm is outstretched. On paper, however, the hand is only a few inches from his brow.

While this problem does not aim specifically at intensifying emotions, foreshortening usually carries that impact. With foreshortening, normal spatial relationships become either compressed or exaggerated, as you can see in Tintoretto's *Lying Man* and Rubens's *Studies of Arms and Legs* (see Figures 9.4 and 9.5).

Rules for figure proportions have been devised over the centuries. Piero della Francesca sometimes spent years working on foreshortened figures in a painting. His treatise *Of the Perspective of Painting*, written sometime between 1480 and 1490, testifies to the extraordinarily complex mathematical limits to which one can go when trying to create the illusion of figures and volumes on a two-dimensional surface (see Figure 9.6). However, with careful looking and translating the rigidity of such formulas can be de-emphasized.

FIGURE 9.3. James Montgomery Flagg: *I Want You*. World War I poster.

FIGURE 9.4. Jacopo Robusti, known as Tintoretto (1518–1594, Venetian): *Lying Man* (ca. 1565). Chalk, 7¼₆″ × 10¹³⁄₁₆″. Art Institute of Chicago.

FIGURE 9.5. Peter Paul Rubens (1577–1640, Flemish): *Studies of Arms and Legs* (ca. 1625). Black chalk heightened with some white, 13¾″ × 9⁷⁄₁₆″. Museum Boymans–Van Beuningen, Rotterdam.

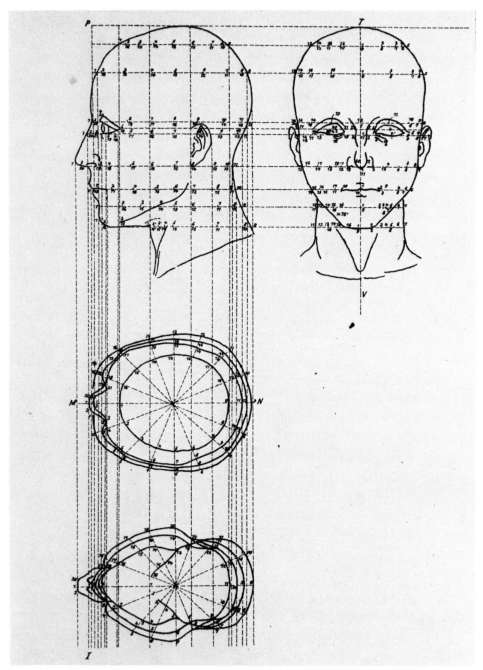

FIGURE 9.6. Piero della Francesca (ca. 1410–1490, Italian): *Man's Head,* from *De prospectiva pingendi* (ca. 1470).

Foreshortening in Contour

With a model seated on a stool on a table and with a vase of dry flowers or weeds alongside, sit on the floor as close to the table as possible. You are looking up. Things will converge to a vertical vanishing point. The composition will have a triangular or a pyramidic shape.

What is the best placement for the composition? More than likely for this exercise, it will be placed vertically on a vertical sheet. But with your particular setup, the composition might need to be drawn horizontally on a horizontal sheet. Place the horizon line, which may be below your paper. Where is the right vanishing point and left vanishing point of the table on that horizon line? The right vanishing point and left vanishing point of the stool? Lay in the composition height, width, and base lines. Then, lay in the vertical/horizontal grid lines very lightly.

Larger masses of flesh are sometimes farther away from you than smaller masses. For instance, thighs and hips will be farther away than calves, if you are seated below the model. Careful scrutiny is needed to maintain proportions; a calf larger than a thigh may well be correct. While "sighting" with your pencil, check the relative scale of feet, legs, thighs, each to the other as they move upward into space. Take a long time "laying in" the establishing lines. Doing this with care will help you become sensitive to proportioning (see Figure 9.7).

To keep proportions accurate, refer to the rungs of the stool or chair on which the model is sitting, or use any reference points you can in the setup you have: the height of the vase, the different heights of the weeds or flowers. Use any reference as often as you need it for calculating foreshortened proportions.

Once the proportions are established by the graphing lines, move back into the drawing with contour line to realize the compressed and overlapping shapes of the figure in its foreshortened point of view. But, just as in linear perspective, once the basic compositional lines and skeletal proportioning are laid in, do not let a compulsion for verisimilitude rob your contour line of information. Your first, though perhaps tentative, lines usually are the more sensitive. Do not feel compelled to erase continually. Sensitivity and dramatic impact are the ends, not mechanical virtuosity. A scratchy contour line can be as uninteresting as a ruled line. Press yourself now to see the characteristics of what it is you are drawing. Surely the line should indicate a difference between wooden stool and human being.

A common difficulty students have with proportion in foreshortening lies in using several perspectives concurrently in the same drawing. One point of view may show the underside of the stool and the model's legs and hips, and then for some reason the point of view shifts and the model is drawn as if from above or from the side. Avoiding that difficulty takes time and concentration, but if you work carefully with the horizontal/vertical measurement lines, that effort should relieve you of awkward mistakes in foreshortening and give you more comprehensive perceptual skills.

The following question is not intended to minimize the impact of Mantegna's work, but can you identify and describe the foreshortening inconsistencies in *The Dead Christ* (see Figure 9.8)? If they do not seem readily apparent, superimpose the horizon line with the vanishing point.

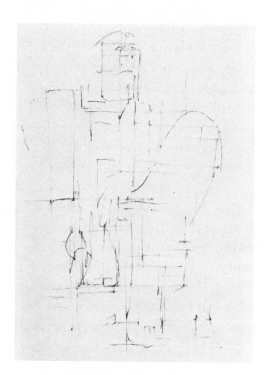

FIGURE 9.7. Establishing lines.

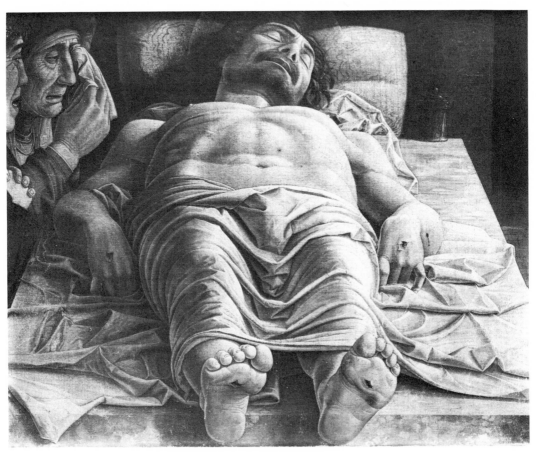

FIGURE 9.8. Andrea Mantegna (1431–1506, Italian): *The Dead Christ* (1570). Tempera on canvas, 26¾″ × 31¾″. Brera Picture Gallery, Milan.

Part Three

THE
GESTURE

FIGURE 10.1. Giacomo Balla (1871–1958, Italian): *Dynamism of a Dog on a Leash* (1912). Oil on canvas, 35″ × 45½″. George F. Goodyear and the Buffalo Fine Arts Academy, New York.

FIGURE 10.2. Eugène Delacroix (1798–1863, French): *Mounted Arab Attacking a Panther* (ca. 1840). Graphic pencil, 9½″ × 8″. Fogg Art Museum, Harvard University, Cambridge, Massachusetts.

FIGURE 10.3. Eugène Delacroix (1798–1863, French): *The Sultan on Horseback* (ca. 1845). Pen and ink. 8⅓″ × 6″. Louvre, Paris.

FIGURE 10.4. Alberto Giacometti (1901–1966, Swiss): *Seated Man* (1953). Pencil, 19¹³⁄₁₆″ × 12¹³⁄₁₆″. Wallraf-Richartz Museum, Cologne.

FIGURE 10.5. Joseph Mallord William Turner (1775–1851, English): *Boats Towing Men-of-War,*
from the *Cyfarthfa Sketchbook* (ca. 1800). Water color, 11½″ × 18″. British Museum, London.

FIGURE 10.6. Auguste Rodin (1840–1917, French): *Standing Nude* (ca. 1900–1905). Pencil and water color, 17⅝″ × 12½″. Art Institute of Chicago.

FIGURE 10.7. Pietro Falca, known as Pietro Longhi (1702–1795, Venetian): *Venetian Wine Shop* (ca. 1750). Pen and brownish wash, 7¾″ × 11⅛″. Private collection.

FIGURE 10.8. Emil Nolde (1867–1956, German): *Harbor* (ca. 1900). Brush and India ink, 12¾″ × 18⅝″. Art Institute of Chicago.

FIGURE 10.9. Ann Poor: *Tying Psycho Patient to a Litter* (1945). Ink and wash, 18⅞″ × 25¹³⁄₁₆″. Art Institute of Chicago.

FIGURE 10.10. Pierre-Paul Prud'hon (1758–1823, French): sheet of studies (ca. 1808). Black ink with brush, Chinese white, and crayon, 11⅜″ × 17⅜″. Art Institute of Chicago.

10

GENERAL GESTURE

Tools
3B or 4B pencil
18" × 24" newsprint pad

Gesture is difficult to explain with precision. Gesture is a translation of the essential characteristics of those shapes you draw. It captures structural rhythm in space, which means linear flow, which in turn means either static or motive energy, which finally means the kinetic abstraction of a whole form. And to add to the difficulty, very often the learning experience in gesture comes *after* you do it.

Up to this point your drawing has been articulated from stable, definitive shapes. Edges as such do not exist in nature, but an arbitrary edge has been used to identify forms in space. If you try to draw a gesture with outer edges, you are missing the point of a gesture drawing. Here is a fast contour, not a gesture (see Figure 10.11).

In beginning stages gesture derives from seeing the structural flow and rhythm of the whole subject matter used. For instance, a lamp (see Figure 10.12).

Observe that these lines do not tell all. Detail is not their objective. They imply. They suggest the interlock of cylinder and cone, the lamp's minimal structural flow. They isolate the linear rhythms of the lamp. Quality in a gesture is elusive. It results from seeing weight, density, thrust, force, stress, and time, factors to be discussed as the problems become more complicated. The point is to embody in lines the *essential*

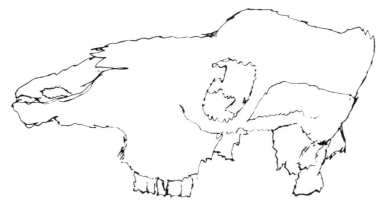

FIGURE 10.11. Skull drawn with a rapid, jerky line.

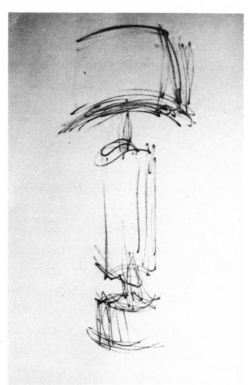

FIGURE 10.12. Lamp drawn in gesture.

characteristics, the structural design, of that whole form you are drawing. Let the characteristics dictate your stroke.

Your first gestures will probably vary in quality, with good informative work in some areas and inconsequential lines in the rest. Of course,
you may be a "lazy looker," focusing more on the paper rather than
studying the object's qualities. Or you may be trying very hard to see,
to understand the problem, but still not be able to transfer the visual
information in gesture. Keep trying. Individuals bring various intuitive
capabilities to their drawing, not to mention preconceptions about what
they think they are seeing. The more you act out drawing, the closer you
will come to the subtle requirements for skilled perception. Rest as-
sured that something authoritative and valuable will happen sooner or
later.

Gesture is an important part of knowing how to draw a figure. For
example, you have to account for the differences in "body English," that
is, the balanced tensions of structure and weight. Drawing literal dimensions is not the objective. Drawing tensions is (see Figure 10.13).

FIGURE 10.13. Student drawing of a figure
in gesture. Pencil on newsprint.

FIGURE 10.14. Student drawing of a figure in gesture. Pencil on newsprint.

FIGURE 10.15. Student drawing of a figure in gesture. Pencil on newsprint.

General Gesture

A gesture of a person is the expressive mass of a figure in space (masses of the head, torso, upper and lower arms and legs). The figure goes all the way around. Try to feel it with your eyes and move your pencil with that feeling, like sculpting with lines.

The illustrations of gesture shown here are individual interpretations (see Figures 10.14 and 10.15). Do not try to copy someone else's translation. See the figure for yourself through gesture because *your* stroke is intrinsic to your own special perceptions.

Problems may arise. The gestures may look like thin, vertical stick figures, active skeletons, wire spring figures, or figures made of balloons. To avoid confusion in general gestures, practice looking at your model for the rhythmic body structure first, then reducing that structure to the five or six most definitive lines. But to reduce those lines to stick figures is too extreme. Your first step will be to interpret the body's major rhythmic lines in simple, informative strokes. Later, you will move into body masses, as if you were building an armature for sculpture.

Working on inexpensive newsprint should encourage exploratory impulses. Draw one sixty-second gesture after another with an eye for the structural flow of the model. Draw those sixty-second gestures for two hours, using any cooperative human being—a kid, a spouse, a friend, whoever will pose.

$$\lceil\ \text{II}\ \rceil$$

ACTION GESTURE

TOOLS
2B pencil or no. 2 conte crayon
newsprint
a model

Leonardo da Vinci was commissioned to paint a mural in the council chamber of the Palazza della Signoria. He chose as his subject the Battle of Anghiari, a famous Florentine battle. *A Rearing Horse* (see Figure 11.1), one of many preliminary drawings, shows gestural experimentation with the tossing head of a horse. Leonardo never finished the fresco for which this drawing was a component sketch. But the cartoon, a full-scale temporary drawing and not now extant, though later copied by Rubens, made Leonardo's final intention apparent. He wanted to freeze the spirit of battle activity in a timeless image rather than to show subjects in action.

One challenge in the early stage of your work is how to capture motion on a sheet of paper. And one good approach to this challenge is to remind yourself that there are different types of motion to be described.

There is the journalistic moment, caught, photographically. Or there is a series of connected motions such as those of a person completing a whole sequence: descending a staircase, playing tennis, jumping hurdles. A synthesis of someone's motion, the Gestalt of that someone's

Action Gesture

walk, is another. Historical time and motion can be compressed into one work, possibly as a montage, which is a series of images super-imposed or arranged in one composition.

The stop-action pose will serve our purpose at this point. The assignment will be to unify three poses into one drawing. The result will not be three separate drawings on one page, but one drawing of three poses within a continuous motion. Motion will be simulated by repetitive images.

Obviously, a live model is needed for this problem. The poses should last about ninety seconds, twenty to thirty seconds for each of the three positions. Advise your model to keep one part of the body stationary so that you can use that part as the pivotal, and somewhat

FIGURE 11.1. Leonardo da Vinci (1452–1519, Italian): *A Rearing Horse* (1504), study for *The Battle of Anghiari*. Red chalk, 6″ × 5⅝″. Royal Library, Windsor Castle, London.

constant, point in the positions you choose. For instance, have the model place one hand on the edge of a stool. First pose: the model kneels, keeping that same hand stationary. Thirty seconds. Draw that pose. Second pose: hand still on the stool, the model stands, bends over slightly, crosses one ankle in front of the other, toe to the floor. Thirty seconds. Draw that pose on the same paper, beginning with the stationary point, the hand. The third pose requires the model's sitting on the stool itself, keeping the hand in the same position. Thirty seconds. Draw that pose on the same sheet of paper beginning with the stationary point, the hand. Your drawing now offers three poses with the hand as the pivotal point.

Before beginning the action drawing, ask the model to demonstrate the whole sequence of the pose so that you can see what kind of space to use for the drawing. For instance, if the three-in-one pose utilizes only seated positions, the best placement on the drawing paper may well be horizontal. If the model poses on a tall stool, the best placement may be on a vertical sheet.

Diagonal poses can be awkward unless you plan your space well. Some diagonal poses work well on a horizontal space, others on a vertical space. There is no hard and fast rule.

Ask the model to try to vary the positions within the full sequence so that the body twists, angles, or in some way makes the pose less static than kneeling, standing straight, and kneeling again. It may be the model who suggests the most creative use of space.

Begin with whatever stationary point the model has established—the hand, the foot, the elbow, the bottom—then move from that point into the drawing (see Figures 11.2, 11.3, and 11.4). Remember that the edges of the figure are not where gesture lies. Gesture lies in exploratory lines which describe the body in motion. Obviously, each body posing will have unique legs, arms, torso, and head. There are always very personal distributions of muscles on bones. Balance points, gravity, and motion are all as uniquely individual as speech variations.

Draw quickly, indicating the most obvious qualities, but avoiding edges. Work from the centers of the limbs and torso outward—first the

FIGURE 11.2. Action gesture, a student drawing of a figure in motion. Pencil on newsprint.

FIGURE 11.3. Action gesture, a student drawing of a figure in motion. Pencil on newsprint.

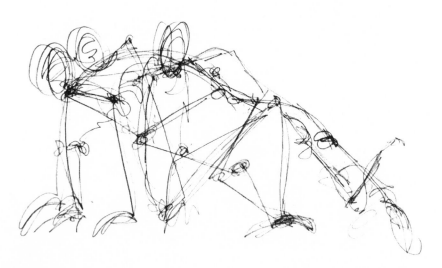

FIGURE 11.4. Action gesture, a student drawing of a figure in motion. Pencil on newsprint.

core, then the mass. Gesture drawing must produce more than a stick figure. If you find yourself still confused about what gesture drawing is, reduce your pencil strokes to the fewest lines that will suggest the most basic rhythmic structure in the model.

Try moving into darker lines for those body areas that sustain the greatest pressure or stress. Feel with your pencil the areas where the body meets resistance as it is leaning or standing or pressing or turning. Lights and darks in this problem indicate variations in weights and pressures. Later, lights and darks will be used as value to produce the illusion of forms in depth.

When you begin to think "rhythmic figure" you will begin to draw rhythmic figure in action.

12

BODY STRESS IN GESTURE

TOOLS
3B pencil or no. 2 conte crayon
newsprint
a model

Drawing body stress in gesture requires the model to assume a body position with as much stress or contortion as possible. The pose should be held until you feel an empathetic response or a sympathetic pain in your own body. For about thirty to forty seconds try holding the same pose as the model's in order to establish a similar pattern of pain in your own body. Then, break the pose and draw the shape of that strain, not as a contour, but as a gesture drawing. Sensing the body as a connected set of stresses, not a connected set of muscles, and drawing what you sense, is the closest you can come to being specific about the stress you are describing in gesture. Don't begin to draw until you *feel* where the model's major stresses are. Begin your drawing by depicting the primary rhythmic force; then build to the rest of the figure.

If you cannot perceive the stress visually, stand up, put yourself into the same position and analyze your set of stresses. Draw the areas that ache. For instance, if you have an area of greater pain over the back of one shoulder than the other shoulder, there is a difference in drawing the gesture shapes of those pains. Move from stress area to stress area in your gesture drawing. Those areas of stress are housed in a unit called

FIGURE 12.1. Body stress drawn in gesture. Ink on newsprint.

the body, obviously, and will assume body proportions, but you are not drawing body per se. Vary the pressure of the pencil by pressing harder where there is more stress and pressing less hard where there is less stress (see Figures 12.1, 12.2 and 12.3).

Gesture drawing refers to sensations as much as perceptions. The student has to sense those interior body signals of stress from the model, most obvious to him or her, and then draw them.

Up until now, the whole concept of gesture has been broken down into exercises, each of which is necessary to the whole. The exercises are similar to clear acetate overlays one finds in encyclopedias of anatomy. One overlay will show a skeletal system, the next a circulation system, the next organs, the next muscles, the next skin.

The early gestures are usually rhythmic lines, establishing the structural flow of the body. Getting more information into the gesture involves discerning where to add another overlay. Moving step by step into action gesture, a student begins to incorporate pressure to suggest areas of stress while at the same time expressing motion through repetitive images. The overlay you are attempting with this problem of stress gesture utilizes all of the information gleaned from the other exercises.

If the gesture problem is still beyond your pencil, go back to drawing the most rhythmic lines indicated in your subject. Continue those until you can glean more information as if you were adding overlays to the human figure. Remember, though, you are not trying to portray anatomical information as such, but to indicate tension and pressure in gesture.

Having reached this stage in a drawing course, some students become exasperated because they feel they do not know what they are doing. They may see others understanding the problems that they just do not "get." These frustrations should not be surprising—and certainly not discouraging. The only answer is: keep trying.

The learning experience for gesture comes after the act. You must do, then discover what you've done. The learning experience in drawing is not an approach to something specific "out there," which when taken step by step will finally be appropriated. Exercises are set up for you to act out through your own selective processes. There are no wrong or right answers. There is only quality or lack of quality. There are excellent, good, and poor drawings, and a textbook can only be a sensitizing tool. You are the instrument, your process is the one that matters.

For this problem of stress gesture, it may ease your approach to use models who can assume poses of stress within actions you know well, for instance stress actions common to baseball, diving, or golf. But the acts of simply pushing on walls, lifting chairs, or pulling on chains are equally informative.

Persevere. Keep on drawing. The revelation, that marvelous "aha" experience, is bound to come if you keep connecting your body-stress sensations to those you perceive in your model, and translating both to your strokes on the paper.

FIGURE 12.2. Body stress drawn in gesture. Conte crayon on newsprint.

FIGURE 12.3. Body stress drawn in gesture. Graphite on newsprint.

13

REVERSE GESTURE

TOOLS
3B pencil or no. 2 conte crayon
newsprint
a model

Reverse gesture is simple to describe, but difficult to execute. Since it is a "sprint" exercise, with your faculties running flat out, a more compressed reasoning comes into play. Drawing a sixty-second mirror gesture takes instant thought-action.

The model should pose so that his or her dominant gesture moves to one side or the other, such as a fencing lunge position. If the lunge is to the right side, that stance should be drawn as if it extended left.

Many of the poses the model might take could spring, again, from gestures in sports—golf, baseball, discus, tennis, curling, to name a few. Some everyday activities will yield good gesture poses for this problem —stepping into a bathtub, turning around, carrying a heavy load on a hip. Actually, any pose that shifts the major body weight more to one side than the other is a workable pose for reverse gesture.

The poses should last no longer than sixty seconds, and you might find that, initially, you cannot fully transpose from what is going left to what is going right. Reverse gesture requires intense, active concentration, and each drawing usually becomes stronger as you work.

After you grasp "reversing," after some twenty or thirty gestures, you also need to look for stress. Vary the pressure of the pencil, pressing harder where there is more stress. And, to complicate things just a little more, try "feeling" with your eyes all the way around the figure. Bodies are cylindrical; they have circumferences. Since some aspects of the body appear to recede, the pencil pressure can be varied accordingly. Firmer strokes for receding areas, lighter strokes for protruding areas.

The fullness of the exercise now is to reverse the model's pose and to vary the pencil pressure according to stresses and masses in the body.

14

GESTURES OF WALKS
AND GESTURAL COMPOSITION

TOOLS
2B pencils
about 80 small pieces of newsprint (4½″ × 6″)
an area where people are walking

The prospect of confronting eighty small sheets of paper is not really as bad as it sounds. For this exercise, tear five sheets carefully, one by one, from an 18″ × 24″ newsprint pad. Cut two or three sheets at a time using a good paper cutter. Cut into four 4½-inch pieces lengthwise, then four 6-inch lengths the other way. That yields eighty 4½″ × 6″ sheets of paper on which to work. Always try to draw on specific sizes of paper. Be careful to make the cuts cleanly and accurately. Torn edges betray sloppy craftsmanship in this problem, and they will confuse the compositional objectives.

In Chapter Eleven the problem of drawing motion was discussed. The three-in-one pose involved a stop-action, repetitive image to indicate motion on a two-dimensional surface.

The drawing of motion in this chapter will encompass the Gestalt of someone's walk. Gestalt is a configuration, the impact of which is greater than the sum of its parts. For our purposes it means the unified physical configuration of motion. In other words, the Gestalt of someone's walk as a drawing will be a single drawing that incorporates as much about a person's walk as you can see and translate. It is unlike the stop-action gesture in that you will be dealing with one image, not three, characterizing a person's total action as he or she walks.

After the paper is cut, the next thing that needs doing is locating a place where you can work comfortably. Narrow hallways are no good. People approach, pass, and go beyond you much too fast.

About twenty yards from a busy sidewalk would do, with pedestrian traffic removed so that you can see your subjects in a lateral, profile motion long enough to draw a Gestalt of their walks. Sometimes library hallways are wide enough to work in. Other options are rotundas, airports, train stations, and downtown streets.

The length of time for viewing a passer-by should vary between four and twenty seconds. In that amount of time, the way a person throws his weight, carries books or packages, places his feet to the ground and rolls off the ball of his foot, the way his clothing flaps in the wind will all need to be seen, assimilated, and put to paper in one drawing. Most of the drawing should be done "blind," that is, by not looking at your paper. In working that way, you are forced to look and look hard at the moving figure.

Usually there are variations in walks. Capitalize on those variations, even to the point of caricature, but *not* to the point of cartoons. The caricature exaggerates the subject's distinctive motions and peculiarities, but doesn't satirize or make judgmental comments visually.

Note from which center the body thrust originates. Some people use their shoulders in a marching rhythm while the rest of their body remains fairly inflexible. Heavier people tend to rotate off the inner tighs, or off their stomachs and bottoms. Some people bounce off the balls of their feet, producing jerky walks that look as if they had an advanced case of hiccups. Pregnant women carry their weight to accommodate the forward displacement.

A person carrying a load of books under his or her arm will compensate for the one-sided weight. Look for the unusual varieties—such as the shufflers, the waddlers, the wide-striders, the tiptoe walkers.

Gestures of Walks

Incorporate parts of clothing, if that helps reveal motion. But you should not, in a ten-second gesture sketch, draw the completely, clothed figure. Far from it. However, if the flair of a skirt is part of the Gestalt, put it in. Or if a distinguishing aspect of the walk involves the flap of a jacket, use it.

Repetition can be used with discretion. If lines that denote repeated motions will reinforce the peculiarity of a person's walk, fine. For instance, a head with massive bobbing hair. But be careful not to slip into cartooning. This problem calls for seeing characteristic aspects of one individual's motions in walking. Be playful in your observation, if necessary, but be serious in your work (see Figure 14.1).

Sometimes a student can work so hard and fast to get down the motion that he or she completely abstracts the motion from the figure. Because the figure houses the motion being drawn, the drawing must

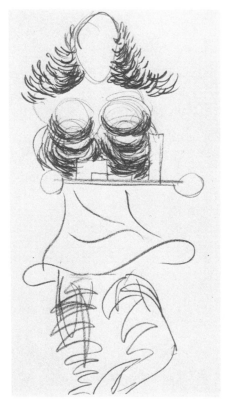

FIGURE 14.1. A student's interpretation in gesture of a waitress walking. Conte crayon on newsprint.

evidence actual aspects of that figure. But the drawings, again, in a gesture exercise are not drawings of complete bodies. They are abbreviated composites.

The walking-gesture problem is frustrating for most persons. If ten or fifteen good drawings emerge out of eighty, that's a good day's work. Even one or two drawings that illustrate a Gestalt, that imply a full human form, and betray motion will justify the effort.

Press yourself to look hard at walks, differentiate your choices as much as you can, and, even when walks are similar, find a uniqueness. Little by little you will begin to see that a few strokes can reveal much information, and that information will depend less on details than on catching signals that indicate a Gestalt (see Figure 14.2).

Gesture compositions are included with this problem because most certainly there will be times when it is not easy to find ambulatory people available to draw. So, when "dry" periods come—that is, when everyone seems to be standing still—use the time to work on compositions (see Figure 14.3).

Within the 360-degree rotation available from a seated position (assuming you are not seated against a wall), there are a number of compositions at hand.

If you are seated some distance from a building, the whole building, including sidewalks, trees, and shrubs, can be used. Zooming in on one area, such as the entryway—which may include railings, lampposts, a sculpture or figures, and landscaping—could be another composition. If that position palls, turn a little. Remember static things carry energy too. Fast contours miss the point. Use gesture.

Formal, centrally placed shapes are usually boring. Sidewalks can easily lead a person's eye off the page. Try counterbalancing lines or shapes that lead one off the page by reinforcing another part of the composition with darker lines. Be careful of the U shapes—archways, circular driveways. They are hard to counterbalance in composition. But draw. It is the way to learn.

The gesture sketch or composition should henceforth precede any drawing you do for several reasons.

FIGURE 14.2. A student's interpretation in gesture of a man running with a racket. Graphite on newsprint.

FIGURE 14.3. Gestural composition of stairs and a doorway.

Gesture sketches can be a shorthand reference to help you choose the best perspective from which to draw. Though gesture compositions can be done quickly, the weight of what they show for your more elaborate efforts is very important.

Also, gesture helps identify the characteristics of mass whether or not that mass is in motion. Gesture implies. Gesture is indeterminate in that edges defining a form dissolve. Gesture characterizes the forms on which you will elaborate with line or value throughout the composition.

The gesture sketch on small pieces of drawing paper and the gestural seeking of forms, once graphing lines are laid down, sustain an expressive life in your work. Avoiding these steps is likely to result in mere copying of lights and darks, which may yield adequate resemblances but misses a responsive vitality that personalizes the translation from eye to hand.

Gesture can also move from its supportive role to become a thing in itself, a species of the genus we might call drawing and painting. If

FIGURE 14.4. Frank Brangwyn (1867–1966, Welsh): *Springtime* (1919). Oil on canvas, 19¾″ × 29½″. Des Moines Art Center.

you draw a gesture sketch with a pencil, you get a gestural line. If you paint a gesture sketch with a brush, you get a gestural stroke. But more than line or stroke, gesture is a way of seeing, a way of thinking about space. Gesture as a mode of drawing and painting will be discussed at length in Chapter Twenty-five. For example, the Welsh painter and etcher Sir Frank William Brangwyn, in his work titled *Springtime* (see Figure 14.4), painted the gentle motion of long grass, girl, and ducks in just such a gestural mode.

Part Four

TRANSITION
INTO VALUES:
VOLUME AND
PATTERN

⌈ 15 ⌉

A PROBLEM IN SCULPTURE—HEADS

Tools
2–3 pounds of non-drying clay
a small cork or styrofoam ball
toothpicks
implements to use in the sculpting process
  (such as small pointed and round
  pieces of metal or wood, spoon handles,
  Q-tips, nail files, etc.)
2 mirrors or 4 photos of you made in a
  photo vending machine—front, sides,
  and back views
a base for the sculpture ($3'' \times 3'' \times 3''$
  block of wood)

Illusion, opposite the eye on a picture plane, is virtual space, meaning space as it appears. The painter or draftsman creates a pretend space for the viewer on a plane. Illusion, or "scene," is not addressed in sculpture, even in bas-relief, so much as volume or mass. The sculptor shapes bulk and makes "tactual space visible." [1] The sculpture, on completion, resides in its own three-dimensional space, enfolded by it (see Figure 15.1). Put another way, sculptural space is what is left of displaced space by the volume of the sculpture. The space surrounding the sculpture should support and complement the volume created. We have cycled back to the unity of positive and negative space.

[*153*]

FIGURE 15.1. Jacob Epstein (1880–1959, English): *Portrait of Albert Einstein* (1933). Bronze, 16¾″ high. Des Moines Art Center.

Seeing and touching is a pause in the drawing sequence to incorporate an experience that, hopefully, will broaden your understanding of volumes—i.e., mass. Working with sculpture moves you to think and work with all the volumes not seen from one point of view in usual drawing practice. When you do draw again, your strokes should be more informed and closer to resolving the deceptive difficulty noted earlier regarding illusion, which is to give assurance of the parts behind and to suggest even what is concealed.

This problem will take anywhere from twelve to forty hours to complete. So once you start, be prepared for a stint. If your work is hasty, it generally looks that way.

The most "known" head you have available is probably your own. You have very distinctive characteristics in the features that comprise your head, and since the problem concerns itself with subtleties, your head is as good as any. Besides, since you always carry it around, you can continue this exercise whenever you have the time.

A Problem in Sculpture

Before starting with the clay, run yourself through a tactile process as follows:

Sit down, close your eyes. With both hands, start at the base of your neck, at the spine, and feel your shoulders. Do they slope gradually below the curvature of the neck? Usually they do. Move back across the shoulders up into the area around your neck. Feel the front lower part of the neck, the part that is scooped out above the clavicles. Move up your throat. What does the cylinder of the esophagus feel like? How far does the esophagus protrude from the muscles at the side of the neck? And where do those muscles connect back down into your shoulders?

Move your hands again to the spinal column in your neck; move up your neck to feel how it curves. Where do the bones recede and the muscles that attach to the skull take over? Feel the bumps in the head right behind the ear. (Most students unnecessarily put overly large lumps of clay at those points on their sculptures.)

Draw your hand down to the connection of the jaw behind the ears. Where are your ears in relation to the bend of the jaw?

Move up the back part of your head. Where does the head start to make it's major curve? Put your thumbs on your ears and rotate your hands to feel all the way up the back of your head. Where does the large curvature peak at the top of your head? For instance, is it at the back center of the skull? From the top center of your head, does the skull curve down, or is it flat for a space and then curve abruptly over your brow line? At the top of the head above the ears, run your hands down to the ears, then into the temples. Does your head narrow at that point? Run the fingers from the temples into the cheekbones, then to the jaw. Do the cheekbones protrude farther than the jaw line?

Is the forehead fairly straight, or is it slanted? How does the brow fit into the temple and cheekbone? Feel the distance between brow and hairline. Run your fingers down over the forehead and feel the bumps in the forehead. Move into the brow line and into the eye. Feel the bone structure of the eye socket. Feel the curvature of the eye and the fleshiness of the eyelid. Feel the inside corner of the eye and how it molds its way back up to the brow and down into the nose. Where is the curvature of the forehead into the nose in relation to the eyeball? At what point does the bridge of the nose extend beyond the brow and the eyeball? Does the flesh of the cheeks exceed the height of the bridge of the nose?

From the bridge of the nose, move fingers of both hands down into the fleshy masses of the cheek and mouth. What is the distance between the upper lip to the base of the nose?

Where are the corners of the mouth in relation to the flair of the nostril and the outer corner of the eye? (Check in a mirror to see if the corners of the mouth are directly below the pupils of the eyes.)

Put your finger vertically to the tip of your nose. Do your lips touch your finger? Put a finger horizontally under your lower lip. How much indentation is there before the chin begins? What is the width of the chin? Wider or narrower than the mouth?

Move down under the chin and feel the flesh that is lying underneath the bone structure. And back into your neck.

The next step in this problem is a scale drawing of your own head, a front view and a side view. The small finished heads measure about four inches in height. With neck and shoulders, they measure about five inches. Using that four-inch measurement on a sheet of scratch paper, begin with a front view of your face, using the front-view photo from the photo vending machine. Adjust the actual physical measurements of your features to the ratio of the four-inch scale. Proceed with grid lines until the general measurements of the face—the brow, the eyes, the nose, the mouth, the chin—are drawn to scale.

Follow the same procedure for a side view, using a photo profile. Take special care with the information around the nose and eyes: eyes rest *behind* the brow; the nose begins to protrude from the curvature at the brow, not from the middle of the forehead. If you draw these small-scale drawings side by side, the horizontal grid lines for the features could be extended from the front-view scale drawing into the side-view scale drawing (see Figure 15.2).

Now you are ready to begin work with the clay. You must build a simple armature, a rough, central framework to support the clay

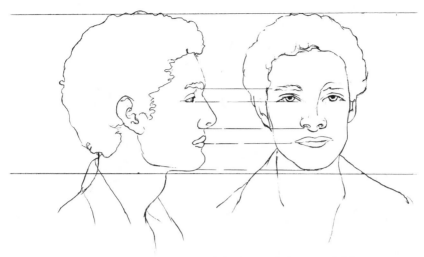

FIGURE 15.2. Scale drawing of a head, front and side.

(see Figure 15.3). Begin by kneading the plasticene clay in your hands and put one layer of it all around the ball. Simulate the neck support by sticking in the four toothpicks (or four small 3″ pieces of thin, stiff wire) closely together in a cluster. The ball will resemble a balloon at this point, but heads are not balloons. Note that a neck tapers at an angle into the head. Try holding the toothpicks at an angle until you have formed a neck-and-shoulder base that will support the head. The head is established as you put the clay up and around the neck onto the cork ball and shape over that cork sphere something closely akin to an egg. The head is not a uniform sphere, so the masses must be shaped over the cork center to conform to the peculiarities of your skull (see Figure 15.3).

Get only the general shape of the head, the brow, the chin, with nothing too detailed. Check the profile in clay against your own in the photo or mirror. Establish the indentation of the nose at the brow and the length and height the nose protrudes. Establish the cheeks.

Working with the eyes is somewhat difficult. Try gouging holes into the clay, putting round balls into them. Then, for the eyelids, place thin layers of clay over the "eyeball" and work the clay flesh into the sockets, cheeks, and nose area.

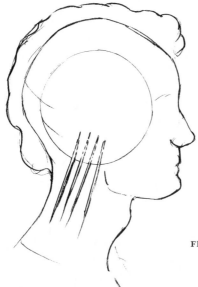

FIGURE 15.3. Simple armature.

FIGURE 15.4. Head, front, a student sculpture.

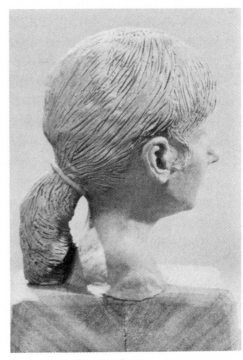

FIGURE 15.5. Head, side.

A Problem in Sculpture

As soon as the large masses are done, put the small head and shoulders down on the stand you will use. From now on work on the sculptured head on its base, rotating the whole unit, head and and base as needed. Nondrying clay gets sticky with too much friction from hands and fingers. Use the sculpting implements you selected to refine and finish the head.

The hair comes last. Hair can be worked in a variety of ways. Some students have used potato mashers through which they press the clay; some make worms; some plait the hair; some comb the clay with a comb; some scratch it with a toothpick. Use your ingenuity.

You will need to check your head and features constantly in the photo or mirror, especially the side view. Often students run into trouble when they build the cheeks puffier than necessary, the chin too far out, the lips puckered, the head resembling a ball instead of an egg, the eyes too far away from the mouth, the nose too long or short, one eye larger than the other. Check yourself in the mirror against your photo. You will be surprised how much you learn about your face.

Since two or three pounds of clay on a small cork-ball–toothpick armature yields a head in miniature, the problem is all the more subtle in terms of pushing masses of clay flesh into the strategic topography of your face and head (see Figures 15.4 and 15.5).

Oil-base clay will dry out somewhat and, inside of one year, begin to crack. But if the work on your sculpture is distinctive and pleasing enough, you may want to retain the small unit temporarily by designing a more permanent base in wood or metal, then pressing the bust to that surface. Completing that, place the sculpture in a space that complements it—in a niche, on a stand by a window, on a library shelf—cognizant of the light and lines surrounding the miniature head.

⌈ 16 ⌉

VALUES IN GESTURE/
THE ELONGATED GESTURE

TOOLS
3B pencil or no. 2 or no. 3 point for
the technical pens
oaktag (about 4 sheets)
the clay head
a model

As added clay builds up on an armature, so the modulating or modeled drawing builds volumes from a rhythmic core. But the modeled gesture builds masses with line, with broken line, or one continuous line moving in as many directions as it takes to build the volumes, indentations, and negatives of what is being drawn.

To "modulate" or "model" in gesture refers to the capability of lines to portray lights and darks. You can accomplish it with two ends in mind. First, lights and darks, drawn with more or less pressure and/ or density, can suggest weight, tension, and stress. Second, lights and darks can indicate the surface pattern of the refraction of light. Moore's *Women Winding Wool* achieves both ends (see Figure 16.1).

Because learning how to modulate values over a surface as the only avenue to drawing is a singularly weak approach, we will begin with a problem similar to the tactile blind contour you did earlier.

Values in Gesture

Without benefit of sight for this first problem in modulating gesture, do a ten-minute blind gesture study of your own head. Draw about life size, feeling your own head with your free hand but using more or less pencil pressure to indicate volumes receding. At the same time move your fingers over and around exploring the sides, top, neck—the topography—of your head, drawing a long, continuous exploratory line. Having sculpted one whole head, now draw as though you were sculpting with line. With two dimensions you will, having meandered over, under, and around your head, have achieved a "simultaneous view," all sides seen at once (which is a concept in Analytical Cubism, discussed in Chapter Twenty-nine).

The second problem in modeled gesture is to use your clay-head sculpture, one view—side or front, and with more or less pencil pressure modulate the long, continuous, meandering line in the drawing according to the light as it bounces off the surface of the clay head. Try a life-sized scale.

Having drawn one long gesture by feeling volumes and one long gesture by observing highlights and shadows, combine the two processes

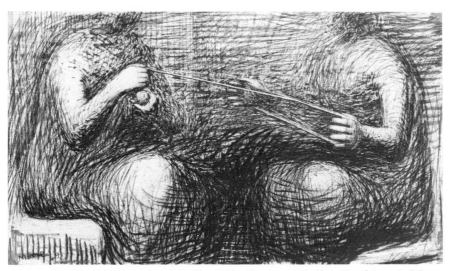

FIGURE 16.1. Henry Moore (b. 1898, English): *Women Winding Wool* (1949). Water color and crayon, 13¾" × 25". Museum of Modern Art, New York.

in the rest of the drawings. While the combination may appear to be the same process, thinking first of volumes and recesses and second of lights and darks builds a very necessary scaffold in drawing.

The third problem will be to work with a model's head, from whatever point of view you have of his or her head.

If you were to wrap thread, string, or a thin wire around the model's head in many directions until you encased it completely, you would have some idea of what modulating gesture is. Features as such should not be delineated, only the masses that designate those features.

Keep in mind the potential use of space on the paper as a composition. Place a head in the middle of the sheet of paper and the composition appears poorly planned. Size of the head in proportion to the size of the paper is important, too. How do you put one head onto a sheet of paper and make a good composition? The question begs your answer.

Keep your pencil to the paper, drawing as you feel your way visually over the model's head. Impart that feeling in your line. Keep reminding yourself that the head is round, its lines go back and around and back again. Gradually the shape of the head will appear. Look at the model more than at the paper. Mentally feel your way up, over, down, around the nose and eyes and ears. Features should be made up of many lines, building up the masses as they intensify and suggest the form. They should not be isolated in contour line.

It is easy to assume that a solution comes by drawing a contour eye, ear, and nose, then wrapping each with a lot of lines. But, the problem does not lie there. You need to feel visually the rise and fall, the heights, widths, depths, lengths, masses, and volumes of the whole head, as though you were a small bug crawling randomly over every inch of space that head had to offer (see Figure 16.2).

The solutions in most of these exercises are helped by the distribution of lights and shadows in that volumes usually correspond with the way light hits the subject's face: lighter lines, more light; darker, more dense lines, less light. But as stated before, drawing stress, weight, or pressure is a subtle way of inferring volumes.

Values in Gesture

FIGURE 16.2. A student
drawing in continuous
gesture. Ink on oaktag.

The fourth problem should be a small drawing (9″ ×12″) of the full figure in modulating gesture. Emphasize stress, mass, and volume. With one long, undulating line try to wrap the form visually as a volume in space (see Figure 16.3).

The fifth problem should be of the whole figure in a simplified setting. Have the model sit on a stool, holding a bowl of flowers, looking out a window, or have her kneeling by a potted plant, but keep it simple.

Indicate the extremities of your composition with the half-inch lines. Using the vertical and horizontal measurements, place the establishing lines for proportion. Then, begin drawing the long, slow, continuous lines, in as many directions and as long as you feel it takes to build the volumes, indentations, and negative of the figure in its simple context (see Figure 16.4).

FIGURE 16.3. A student drawing in value gesture. Graphite on newsprint.

FIGURE 16.4. A student drawing in continuous gesture with values. Ink on white drawing paper.

⌈ 17 ⌉

THREE-TONE PATTERN
IN CONTOUR

TOOLS

2B pencil
18″ × 24″ sheet of oaktag
2 small bottles
1 color of ink plus white and black
several small brushes
a setup with a model, or a still life

We come now to the last of three transitional chapters. We have worked with literal volumes in sculpture, then with suggested volumes in the elongated gesture relating lights and darks to stresses and weights as well as to surface light refractions. Our task at this stage is to encase flat shapes of light tones, middle tones, and dark tones with contour lines, establishing patterns that will also *infer* volume.

In a sense this exercise corresponds to the stages of spatial development, in figures on Greek vases. The full development of the Geometric phase of Greek art, ca. 800 B.C., produced pottery with solid black figures on terra cotta (see Figure 17.1). The figures were generally flat and ornamental, employing repeated chevrons, circles, and dots. There were no shadows.

The Orientalizing period of Greek vase painting, ca. 700–620 B.C.,

FIGURE 17.1. Attic: Dipylon vase (eighth century B.C.). 42½" high. Metropolitan Museum of Art, New York.

showed humanized figures, usually silhouetted (see Figure 17.2). Sometimes only a contour outline was drawn. Sometimes a combination of both approaches is seen. Artisans incised lines into the black glaze on the pottery to identify arms, drapery, etc. White or purple glaze was added on top of the black glaze to make some areas appear to protrude.

In Archaic vase painting of ca. 600–480 B.C., there was a gradual change from black to red figures (see Figure 17.3), the figures freely drawn with line rather than laboriously incised, incorporating foreshortening and overlapping limbs. The Greeks were thus using line, value, and color to give the illusion of a limited, but receding space.

With this three-tone exercise, you are asked to reutilize contour and at the same time incorporate value and color, much as the Greeks of fifth century B.C. The use of outlined flat value shapes—lights, middles, and darks—can suggest a limited recession into space.

Drawing from a still life or model in a setup, the basic concern in this exercise is to *flatten* space to patterns by drawing distinct, unmodulated, closed value shapes. When the drawing of the value-shape patterns is completed, a viewer's eye will know, nevertheless, that

FIGURE 17.2. The Arkesilas Painter: Laconian cup (ca. 565–560 B.C.). Pottery, 7¹³⁄₁₆″ height, 14¹⁵⁄₁₆″ diameter. Bibliothèque Nationale, Paris.

FIGURE 17.3. Douris: *Eos and Memnon* (ca. 490–480 B.C.). Interior of an Attic red-figured kylix, 10½″ diameter. Louvre, Paris.

dimension or volume is there. The viewer will make associations with actual still lifes or figures even though what you devised was merely an illusion based on flatness.

Actually, there can be two and one half to three feet of physical depth in a setup involving a human body. But individual objects, the model, the drapery, whatever you use in the setup will appear flattened when you deny the object its own shape and see the whole series of objects and background only as flat value shapes.

Prepare the setup, ready the model, turn on a floodlight (possibly in a darkened room), draw several gesture sketches for composition, then select the most interesting point of view from those sketches. Lay out on your paper the general composition and establishing lines in pencil, then squint. Remember, squinting causes the value shapes to appear more distinct.

Decide as you scan the setup what and where your lightest value shapes are. Is the lightest value shape of a gray drapery equivalent to the lightest value of the reflected light shape on a shiny glazed brown bottle? Will the whites, off-whites, light grays, light browns all be the lightest value shapes or will some of them move into a middle-tone shape?

Remember, you are *not* drawing objects and coloring them in. You are drawing value shapes, and a light value shape may well encompass parts of two or more adjacent items in the setup. The shine of a bottle, the curvilinear value of a drapery, and a highlighted portion of the model's hair could all be one enclosed shape, a light value.

For a moment now, turn and look at objects and figures in your room. You will see a wide scale of values. Light modulates with more variations than merely highs, middles, and lows. There are highlights, middle lights, middle-middle lights, middles, mid-darks, darks, dark-darks, down the line. This problem requires an arbitrary judgment of light, middle, and dark values. Each of the shapes drawn will be only one of three values. There should be no transient modulation.

By encompassing the whole compositional space with closed, flat shapes, by reducing all the space to a flat pattern in shapes of three values, you are manipulating visual space purposefully. This kind of

Three-Tone Pattern in Contour

drawing will take you away from copying objects and move you another step toward translating (see Figure 17.4).

First, identify and draw in all the lightest value shapes you can see. Draw with contour line and close the shape completely.

Then, scan the setup for all the darkest shapes, remembering that the shadow of a foot may be equivalent in value to the color of the unlighted value shape of the stool leg, and both may become one shape in the darkest value.

The remaining shapes automatically become the middle value shapes.

At the risk of sounding like a paint-by-number kit, some system needs to be devised to keep the values identified, so that later when you are duplicating the values in colored ink, you will be able to know which is which. Insert either numbers (1, 2, 3) or letters (L, M, and D). The problem does have a certain "coloring book" onus; but at this stage, coloring in shapes is still part of a learning process.

To finish the work, almost any color ink—blue, red, orange, sepia, green, purple—will do. You will also need black and white.

FIGURE 17.4. A student three-tone drawing using sepia and India ink on oaktag.

FIGURE 17.5. A student three-tone drawing using orange, white, and India ink on oaktag.

FIGURE 17.6. A student three-tone drawing using persimmon, white, and India ink on oaktag.

FIGURE 17.7. A student three-tone drawing using red, white, and India ink on oaktag.

Three-Tone Pattern in Contour

The colored ink you choose will be your middle value. Into a small jar, pour some of the colored ink plus enough white ink to change the middle value color to a light value color. Pour in enough of both so that you can fill all the light value shapes with one batch of mixed light value.

Into another small jar, pour some of the colored ink plus a little black ink to change the middle value color to a dark value color. Mix sparingly. Black ink quickly and substantially darkens colors. Pour in enough of each so that you can fill all the dark value shapes with one batch of mixed dark value.

Some colors of ink cover better than others. If you selected a color that doesn't spread consistently, it might be useful to go over the shapes twice.

Within your original contour shapes, the drawing should be completely inked with individual color values. Follow the value code system you've established, numbers or letters, and correspond the ink values to those identified, closed shapes. Ink is best applied with a brush, but can be done with a wide Speedball pen point. Fill the shapes in ink from one side of the paper to the other side and from top to bottom (see Figures 17.4, 17.5, 17.6, and 17.7).

This particular exercise was developed to encourage the abstraction of like values throughout the whole composition, regardless of the objects. Values become the shapes, albeit flattening the space to patterns, but still surprisingly suggestive of depth.

The three tone, the modeled values in gesture done earlier, and the value studies in the next chapters—all are guiding you toward the illusion of depth. However, drawing as an expressive form need not rest finally on the illusion of depth. For centuries Western art trained our sensibilities to expect that the appearance of the real world is the appropriate concern of the arts. Even this collection of beginning exercises is generously imbued with the philosophy of perspective or depth illusion. But you should regard these kinds of spatial problems simply as a preliminary part of your visual training.

Part Five

VALUE

FIGURE 18.1. Claude Lorrain (1600–1682, French): *The Tiber above Rome, View from Monte Mario* (ca. 1640). Brush and bistre wash, 7⅜″ × 10⅝″. British Museum, London.

FIGURE 18.2. Odilon Redon (1840–1916, French): *The Reader* (1892). Lithograph, 12³⁄₁₆″ × 9⁵⁄₁₆″. Sotheby Parke Bernet, London.

FIGURE 18.3. Ignace Henri Joseph Théodore Fantin-Latour (1836–1904, French): *Bouquet of Roses* (1879). Lithograph, 16⁵⁄₁₆″ × 13⅞″. Des Moines Art Center.

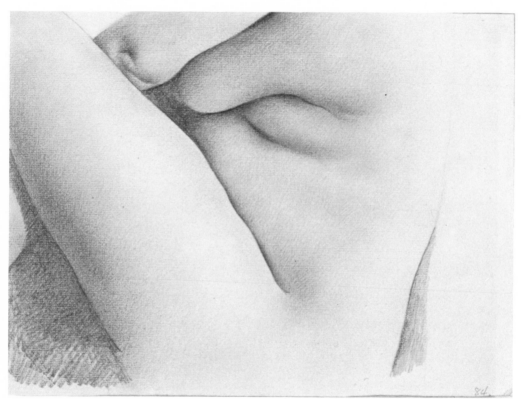

FIGURE 18.4. Charles Sheeler (1883–1965, American): *Nude Torso* (ca. 1924). Pencil, 4½″ × 6⁵⁄₁₆″. Art Institute of Chicago.

FIGURE 18.5. Pieter Cornelis Mondriaan (1872–1944, Dutch): *Trees by the River Gein* (ca. 1902). Charcoal, 18⅜″ × 24½″. Art Institute of Chicago.

FIGURE 18.6. Francesco Guardi (1712–1793, Italian): *Adoration of the Shepherds* (ca. 1750). Pen and ink with brown and gray wash over red chalk, 15¼″ × 20⅜″. Art Institute of Chicago.

FIGURE 18.7. Mary Cassatt (1845–1926, American): *Nicolle and Her Mother* (ca. 1900). Pastel, 25⅛″ × 20¾″. Des Moines Art Center.

FIGURE 18.8. Jean-Baptiste Carpeaux (1827–1875, French): *Seated Woman* (ca. 1850). Black and white chalk, 8⅞″ × 6⅛″. Art Institute of Chicago.

FIGURE 18.9. Georges Seurat (1859–1891, French): *The Artist's Mother Seated before a Window* (ca. 1882). Black crayon over traces of brown ink, 6¼″ × 4¾″. Metropolitan Museum of Art, New York.

FIGURE 18.10. Berthe Morisot (1845–1895, French): *Self-Portrait* (1885). Pastel, 18″ × 14″. Art Institute of Chicago.

⌐ 18 ⌐

VALUE STUDIES

Tools
vine charcoal and compressed charcoal
  or black chalk
white or cream-colored charcoal paper
newsprint

Because light rays bounce from points on a subject to points on the retina of the eye, our mind perceives an image. We see every opaque unit surrounded with light, more or less, according to the intensity and direction of the light source. Shadow is the obstruction of light and is seen in stages, as is light. The scale of gradations between light and dark is called a value scale (see Figure 18.11). A value will vary in brightness or dullness (intensity) and lightness or darkness relative

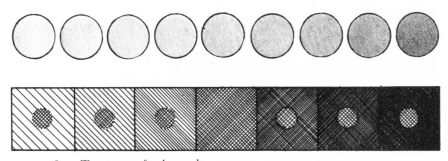

FIGURE 18.11. Two types of value scales.

[*185*]

to an adjacent value. Light gray will look lighter and brighter next to black, darker and duller next to white.

A color value finder would help you match a color to its equivalent gray. Small holes perforate each gray square of gradation. Squinting through the perforations, matching the color of the thing you see to its equivalent gray value, helps identify monochromatic (one color) lights and darks to be translated in a drawing.[1]

Escher's *Drawing Hands* (1948) illustrates systematic value changes (see Figure 18.12). Identification of the gradations is fairly simple:

> *highlight*—the lightest area;
> *light*—the next lightest area;
> *half tone*—from mid-light to mid-dark;
> *core tone*—the most concentrated area of darkness;
> *reflected light*—light deflected from another surface;
> *cast shadow*—thrown by the object obstructing light.

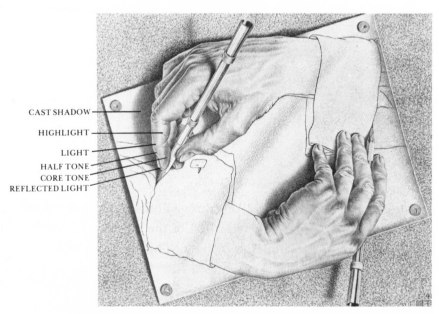

FIGURE 18.12. M. C. Escher (1898–1972, Dutch): *Drawing Hands* (1948). Lithograph, 11¼″ × 13⅜″. Gemeentemuseum, The Hague.

Value Studies

The usual procedure in drawing is applying dark strokes to light paper. The continuous monochromatic gradations between highlights and deep darks was called chiaroscuro in the seventeenth century. The sixteenth-century interpretation of the Italian words *chiaro,* "light," and *oscuro,* "dark," meant something else. *Chiaro oscuro* described a method of working on a middle-tone support, using white to define the forms in a drawing. The dark tones became almost secondary in importance to the dramatic contrast with the whites used. The middle tone of the paper served as the middle tone for the modeling process between the atmospheric lights and the dark shapes shrouded in shadows.

In this chapter you are asked to draw with a range of values from highlights to deep darks, a chiaroscuro problem. But to avoid confusion the problem is described simply as "value study."

Values are used to help identify volumes in space. This means they codify colors in grays, and they reinforce perspective or spatial references. Values lend dynamics to a drawing; they yield impact and mood.

A student must learn the subtleties of value relationships to produce convincing work. Whether a subject is drawn with values at the light end of the scale, at the dark end of the scale, or with the full range of values, white to black, the information perceived through the eye should sustain what has already been structured and drawn— namely, the disposition of volumes in space. The disposition of volumes embodies both the gestural characteristics derived from the object and the object's basic geometric form (a bottle as a cylinder, for example). A broader description and exercise treats geometric forms in Chapter Twenty.

Just as in the three-tone, like values will first be abstracted throughout the whole composition regardless of the objects as a way to sensitize your eye to the subtleties of light. This chapter emphasizes local values, or values as they appear. The next chapter emphasizes reverse values, with lights inverted as darks and darks inverted as lights. And Chapter Twenty introduces you to drawing geometric forms on which values are stroked.

Once again, the problem is to see and draw like value shapes through-out the composition regardless of separate items. This exercise, how-ever, will take you a step further in that after the value shapes are drawn, modeling follows. Modeling requires blending, maintaining constant reference to the subject being drawn while fusing lights into middle tones, middle tones into dark tones, and dark tones into very dark shades.

A bottle is easy to see just as an object. But, isolating objects and coloring (or, in this case, graying) them in misses the point of this exercise. Objects occupy space. Unfortunately, sometimes an isolated object "looks good," and the beginner is convinced that rendering isolated objects is enough (see Figure 18.13).

But the scope of good drawing is far more complex. What happens in a drawing to the space that surrounds all objects? Negative space needs to be resolved with the positive shapes. Drawing each unit separately keeps a drawing incomplete. Defining systematic value changes, first as flat pattern shapes, then modeling them into volumes and voids throughout the whole still life should ease you toward a more secure aesthetic space.

Set up a still life with a single light source. As you are setting up, take mental note of the weights, the materials, the masses or bulks, the textures, and the colors of the arranged items. Those components affect light differently, and the differences should be noted for later use.

Draw several small gestural sketches from different points of view. Select the sketch that seems the strongest in composition, and station yourself where you drew that sketch. Now, on a fresh sheet of paper, lay in the establishing one-half-inch lines for proportioning.

Proceed to the value shapes. Sit looking at the still life a minute or so while squinting your eyes. The highest lights and the darkest darks should stand out. Squinting off and on throughout your drawing process will help define the perimeters of a value shape.

With the six value gradations in mind, scan the whole still life for each value grouping each time—the highlights, the lights, the half

FIGURE 18.13. A bottle drawn as an isolated shape. Charcoal on white drawing
paper.

FIGURE 18.14. A student drawing of a
still life with value shapes left as planes.
Charcoal on charcoal paper.

tones, the core tones, the reflected lights (if any), and the cast-shadow
shapes. Remember, the half-tone on a bottle may be equivalent in
value to a core tone in the adjacent pale-blue drapery. Consider that
as one value shape.

The color of your paper is the lightest value, synonymous with highlight. If the still life contains no highlights (intense lights) the color
of the paper is synonymous with the next lightest value, the light tone.
The next lower tone shapes will be the ones you begin to draw across
your paper as they appear throughout the still life. Seek, then, each
group of gradations within the still-life unit at successive drawing
steps. Once those stages are complete, the drawing will look flat and
patterned (see Figure 18.14). Your drawing is a sequence of planes.

However, a drawing left this way remains relatively flat. Begin now
to manipulate the charcoal value shapes by smearing them together,
using your fingers, a paper stick, a small chamois, or a soft paper
towel. Refer back to the still life continually as you move one value

FIGURE 18.15. A student drawing of a still life integrating value shapes with volumes. Charcoal on white drawing paper.

FIGURE 18.16. A student drawing of a still life integrating value shapes throughout the composition. Charcoal on newsprint.

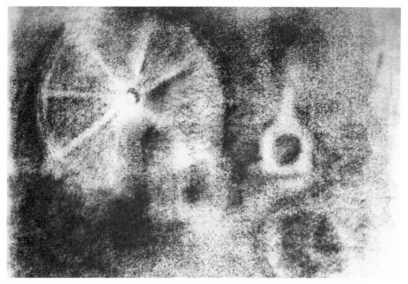

FIGURE 18.17. A student drawing of a still life inferring depth. Charcoal on charcoal paper.

Value Studies

into another. Work the middle tones into the light tones, creating light middle values. Push the middle tones into the core tones, creating dark middle values. (The core tones can be made darker by changing from vine charcoal to compressed charcoal.) Values should now bring to life the weights, the materials, the textures, and the volumes within the still-life setup.

Eventually, your drawing will have items and space that appear approximate to the still life. You have achieved it through a scrutiny of values, a manipulation of positives and negatives, and exploration of such factors as weight and texture (see Figures 18.15, 18.16, and 18.17).

REVERSE VALUE STUDIES

Tools
black charcoal paper
white and gray chalk

You will find that working on black paper differs from working on white paper in that toned papers require more opaque drawing and will weaken value contrasts. The "ground," loosely meaning the surface (white or toned) on which a drawing or painting will be executed, is carefully chosen by artists. Technically, "ground" means what prepares a support surface whether that surface is a wall, a canvas, or a sheet of paper. Typical grounds are thin glue or chalk or plaster and gelatin mixed with water. Among their uses, grounds provide a consistent surface and subtly influence colors and values used in a drawing or painting.

One of the distinguishing characteristics of the Pre-Raphaelites, a group of young English painters in the 1850s, was a particular luminosity achieved by painting on a wet, very white ground. Michelangelo sometimes used a light-green earth wash as ground. Leonardo recommended white. The Venetians favored dark grounds such as brown or brownish reds. The Florentines prefered light-gray grounds.

The black "ground" you are working on in this problem will influence or show through every stroke you put on the paper. But part of this problem is meant to test the potentials of the materials in your drawings.

Reverse Value Studies

Conventional value, sometimes termed *local value,* can be defined as reflected light seen naturally. Such value is a routine feature in most drawing and painting. Reverse value does not imply a different reflection of light. Reverse value means, very simply, the inversion of lights for darks and darks for lights. By using a dark ground and by reversing values, new value dynamics emerge. Mood suddenly becomes evident. Drawings seem strangely eerie. Even though you draw a sunlit pine tree, by reversing the values—making the trunk light and the needle tips dark—you have created a peculiarly evocative image.

Reverse value is a good outdoor problem on a very sunny day, when light contrasts are sharp. Extreme values are easier to see when the lighting is intense. Find an interesting place in a park, on a farm, on an open street, wherever. Having selected a composition from several small gesture sketches, return to that point of view and sit comfortably. Using black paper and white or gray chalk, lay in the half-inch perimeter and establishing lines for a good composition. Remember the horizon line and imply it on your paper with dots or a line so that your perspective principles remain consistent.

Look at the lightest values, the highlights—those will be the value of the black paper. Begin drawing the next lightest shapes, the light tones. Scan the scene, selecting only the light tones; then draw them throughout your whole composition as the next darkest shapes. Let the blackness of the paper permeate the gray chalk to achieve the values you need. Then draw the next lightest shapes, the half tones, remembering always to reverse the local value. The middle-tone shapes will retain the same values on either a white or black ground. Placed alongside each other, middle values on black and white grounds will appear different because of the medium and the ground—but their "gray values" are roughly equivalent.

Drawing the lightest value shapes first over the whole composition repeats the process the previous exercise called for. But this time, by reversing the effect, you are also refining and condensing your concentration much as you did with reverse gesture and inverted contour.

Working with a soft medium such as chalk, you will need to push, smear, and blend the values to obtain the soft, modulated chiaroscuro

FIGURE 19.1. A student drawing of a hallway using reverse value. White chalk on black charcoal paper.

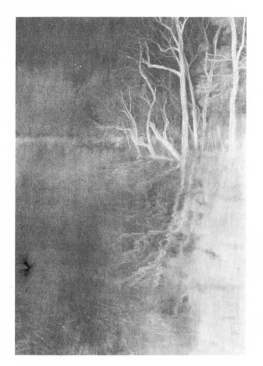

FIGURE 19.2. A student drawing of a landscape using reverse value. White chalk on black charcoal paper.

Reverse Value Studies

that creates the illusion of depth. Since values are reversed and perhaps volumes also, does depth appear reversed too? Lights are known to come forward and darks to recede. Or, does your drawing suggest depth the same way a drawing with local or natural values would, maintaining conventional volumetric shapes? By reversing values, have our natural instincts with space been teased into perceiving another dimension, a somewhat mysterious space/time suspension (see Figures 19.1 and 19.2)?

Values are an interesting phenomenon. Understanding the subtleties of value is very important, but just as with the other elements of drawing, values do not stand alone easily at this stage of drawing. Abstracting the geometric structure of volumes over which you stroke values is the next prerequisite toward expressive drawing.

⌐ 20 ⌐

VALUE IN DRAPERY

TOOLS
gray, brown, or slate-blue charcoal paper
white and gray pastels
            or
white or off-white charcoal paper
charcoal
paper stick

You remember that Brunelleschi, an architect of the *quattrocento* (Italian for the 1400s), helped formulate the principles of linear perspective. Most artists of that period were committed to achieving the appearance of depth or volume. They studied the works of classical Greece (ca. 500–200 B.C.) because they believed the Greeks had realized near perfection in idealized proportion, expression, and form. Artists throughout the Italian Renaissance strived to combine Brunelleschi's principles of illusory depth with Greek classical models using scientific accuracy and systematic methods to precipitate an ideal beauty.

Because the Greek and Italian artists both worked with figures, drapery was an attendant problem. The artists of each time chose to unify the body with the material. The natural fall of the drapery became important (see Figure 20.1).

FIGURE 20.1. Lorenzo di Credi (ca. 1458–1537, Italian): *Saint Bartholomew* (ca. 1510). Pencil, white and red chalk on brown paper, 15¹³⁄₁₆″ × 10⅝″. Louvre, Paris.

From Athens to Florence, the figure and its drapery had passed through one thousand years of interpretation by different artists from different schools in different countries before systematic standards of beauty were to resurface. And just as the Florentines looked to Greece for aesthetic information, we look to the Renaissance Florentines.

Among systematic standards are geometric volumes which can be classified as the cube, the cone, the cylinder, the sphere, the rectangular box, the pyramid, and the prism. Every volume you see, natural or man-made, can be reduced to its equivalent cubic unit: tree trunks and limbs become clusters of cylinders; houses become cubes or rectangular boxes; hills become half spheres; a nose becomes a pyramid, a smaller volume of a larger volume, the head, a sphere. (Paul Cézanne felt that all natural forms were based on the cone, the sphere, and the cylinder—to put a complex theory simply.) Because the direction and mass of the forms are hard to analyze, a beginning student often miscalculates depth in such a way that things appear flat. Graphing lines will help establish height and width, but the abstracting of geometric volume will guide you with depth perception. What the eye sees is processed in the mind. If a volume is naturally three feet deep but drawn as though it were a plane, the perception translated into the drawing is inconsistent with the information given. In the long, early stages of drawing, as a matter of course, thinking through and sketching in all the volumetric shapes within a composition before values are applied is a process that reaps expressive benefits later.

The drawing of drapery by itself is a simple way of learning how to reduce volumes to geometric structures. Drapery lends itself well to this kind of reduction because the volumes within the drape, the folds of the cloth, can easily be translated to cones or pyramids.

Begin by draping several different materials—wide or long, heavy or lightweight. Try several arrangements. Burlap and silk hang differently. Velvet and leather hang differently. Material shiny on one side and dull on the other is excellent for identifying volumetric shapes. Thumbtack or pin the drapery across a wall or a bulletin board, or hang one on a coatrack, or drape one over a tree limb—whatever works

Value in Drapery

best. Some artists have dipped material in plaster, arranged the folds, let the material dry, and then drawn studies. Experiment long enough while hanging the drapery in order to create a complex variety of folds.

Drawing drapery tends to exacerbate two problems in composition—namely, running off the page and/or "hanging" in space. If the drapery is long, heavy, and horizontally hung, you may find that the repeated U shapes are boring and move the eye in a wavelike motion off the page. That shortcoming can be compensated by selecting the most interesting portion of the drapery to draw, then vignetting the edges. This means smearing some of the edges to fade into the surrounding negative space, suggesting the total piece of drapery. The composition is resolved in that the image appears to be complete and rests within a stable space.

On several sheets of small paper, draw one- or two-minute gesture sketches to find the best composition. Then from the best, select your point of view and lay out the perimeters of the general composition. Lay in proportions with establishing lines. Do not forget the horizon line. The analysis should be a slow, detailed process as you begin drawing the geometric volumes. Work lightly with your pencil, using contour lines to identify not what you see, but the abstracted geometric volumes of what you see. If you cannot identify geometric structure in the drapery from your point of view, go up to the material and look more closely at the points where convex folds begin to curve under and concave folds are thereby formed. Back at your point of view, observe how light articulates the ins and outs of the volumes, helping you to identify the geometric sub-structure, made up of long pyramids or cones. After the geometric structures are drawn with light contour lines, study the play of light on the drapery and establish value in your drawing as you did in the previous chapter.

By now you should understand that one of the most critical components of composition is value. How well value supports what is already drawn depends, of course, on your eye and hand. Stroking values over the scaffolding of geometric volumes can be done in a number of ways, but of primary importance is that you understand the subtle

FIGURE 20.2. A student drawing of the structure of drapery over which values were stroked.

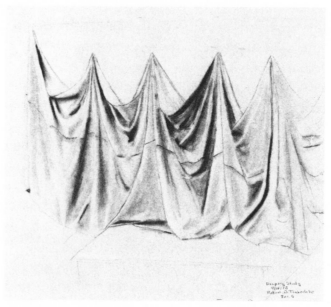

FIGURE 20.3. A student drawing of the structure of drapery over which values were stroked.

Value in Drapery

interplay of value changes throughout the composition. Hurrying does not breed sensitivity.

If laying out the whole pattern of value shapes from highlight to shadow works well for you, continue working that way. If you want to model values as you proceed, keep an eye on the compositional unity of the drawing. But the moment you feel you are coloring objects, stop drawing, go back to identifying each group of like values through the whole composition, and then model one value into another. Remember to check for the darkest values, the core tones, the reflected light shapes, and the cast shadows from one fold of drapery onto another.

You might want to try working from the dark values up to the color of your white paper. If you are using a middle-tone charcoal paper (gray, brown, or slate blue), you could move your values down to black for the darkest areas, up to white for the lightest areas and use the color of your paper for the middle tones (a contemporary version of sixteenth-century chiaro oscuro). The paper stick, a cylinder of compressed soft paper, could be employed cautiously to smear or smudge either charcoal or chalk. A small chamois or your fingers would do much the same thing (see Figures 20.2 and 20.3).

The lengths to which artists have gone to draw the natural fall of drapery can be seen in Mantegna's drawing, *St. James Led to His Execution* (see Figure 20.4). The body was drawn first, then draped.

In addition to the formal structuring of drapery, artists often used drapery to identify or support the character of their subjects. Sometimes the drapery is arranged and handled in such a way as to have a life of its own, regardless of the figure wearing it. The use of drapery shown by the formal arrangement of line, volume, value, texture, and composition is distinctly unique in each of the following chronological illustrations (see Figures 20.5, 20.6, 20.7, 20.8, and 20.9).

FIGURE 20.4. Andrea Mantegna (1431–1506, Italian): *St. James Led to His Execution* (ca. 1455). Pen drawing, 6⅛″ × 9¼″. British Museum, London.

FIGURE 20:5. The Master of Flémalle (Robert Campin?): *The Merode Altarpiece*, center panel (ca. 1425–1428). Oil on wood, 25³⁄₁₆″ × 24⅞″. The Cloisters Collection, Metropolitan Museum of Art, New York.

FIGURE 20.6. Alessandro di Mariano dei Filipepi, known as Botticelli (1445–1510, Italian): *The Three Graces,* detail from the *Primavera* (ca. 1478). Tempera on wood panel. Uffizi Gallery, Florence.

FIGURE 20.7. Johannes Vermeer (1632–1675, Dutch): *Artist in His Studio* (ca. 1665–1670). Oil on canvas, 52″ × 44″. Kunsthistorisches Museum, Vienna.

FIGURE 20.8. Jean-Auguste-Dominique Ingres (1780–1867, French): *Napoleon As Emperor* (1806). Oil on canvas, 8′ 7″ × 5′ 5″. Musée de L'Armée, Paris.

FIGURE 20.9. Gustave Doré (1832–1883, French): *Scripture Reader in a Night Refuge,* from *London: A Pilgrimage* (ca. 1870). Wood engraving, 9⅚₁₆″ × 7½″.

21

SAME SUBJECT—
THREE LIGHTING POSITIONS

Tools
3 9″ × 12″ light- or middle-tone
  charcoal sheets
charcoal pencil
paper stick
several sheets of newsprint

Working with values only at the dark end of the scale, the light end of the scale, or in the middle of the scale, each is an exercise in subtle observation. In this case, dark tones will be used—the shadow, the core tone, and the cast shadow.

Dark value shapes drawn and modeled tend to infer volumes not drawn. The light- and middle-tone shapes not drawn at all then become negative shapes. But because those negative shapes are bounded by dark modulated values, the negatives take on the appearance of volumes in concert with the shadows. The shadow shapes will change as the lighting positions change, but, since you remain in one position, the volumes inferred by the shadows do not change (see Figures 21.1, 21.2, and 21.3).

The vast range of possibilities in seeing and translating should become increasingly apparent as you move through these exercises. Years of experimentation with still life would hardly exhaust the technical possibilities, let alone the philosophical or theoretical ones. The same subject matter you choose for this problem could be drawn with light values or middle values. The light source could vary 30 degrees each time. You could choose any medium, any color, any paper. Choice is a signal factor. You grow in your work as your choices are refined. For arbitrary purposes let's work with the lower registers of values.

A still life is probably the best subject matter to use for this problem. A darkened room and a spotlight (or some other single light source such as a small desk lamp) are necessary. Shoes, bottles, vases, flowers, dry weeds, parts of old machines, almost any group of objects with defined shapes casting definite shadows will work as components for the still life. However, there are limits to usability; a limp pile of clothing, for instance, will not prove very suitable by itself.

The point of view will remain the same for each of these drawings. To find that point of view you will need to draw several gesture sketches of the still life from different positions. Study the sketches and select the best.

After you select the stable point of view, experiment with the light and decide on the three positions you will use for your light-source placement. Far left, middle, far right; left, overhead middle, right; or left, low middle, and right are possible combinations.

From your point of view now draw a five- or ten-minute study of the dark value shapes on fresh 5″ × 7″ sheets of newsprint for each lighting placement. See if the patterns of the value shapes work as well for each composition as the gesture did. If the values can stand alone as a strong composition, move to the charcoal paper. Otherwise, find a different point of view or different positions for the light.

Using one of the three 9″ × 12″ sheets of charcoal paper, very lightly lay out the composition in half-inch perimeter and establishing lines for the first light position. Very lightly let your gesture now identify the characteristics of the volumes you will be drawing. The gesture should be drawn light enough to erase, or executed by the motion of your hand without a drawing utensil. Even without something to mark your paper, the information eye to hand informs the strokes you will make.

Now squint. Select and draw only the dark shapes, the shadows, the core tones within the shadow, and the cast shadows. This will leave your composition full of light tones and middle tones, which become one large negative shape, the color of your paper. If you place the dark shapes strategically in the drawing and, with the paper stick or a finger, modulate those dark volumes with enough sensitivity, you should have shapes that imply all of the volumes. Repeat the process for the other two light positions (see Figures 21.1, 21.2, and 21.3).

FIGURE 21.1. Light source to the left.

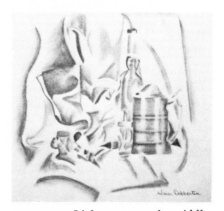

FIGURE 21.2. Light source to the middle.

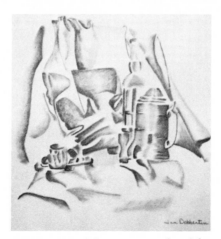

FIGURE 21.3. Light source to the right.

22

CROSSHATCH

TOOLS
middle-tone construction paper
white and black colored pencils
still life or a model in a setup
spotlight or strong natural light

Crosshatch is a method of working in value that uses a series of short, sometimes profuse, intersecting parallel lines to build a composition of volumes and negatives.

Crosshatching, often used in intaglio printing processes (see Figures 22.1, 22.2, 22.3, and 22.4), illustrates that the process needs to be an integral part of the subject as it is finally presented. The process, materials, image, and subject are unified in each of the prints. (Definitions between *subject* and *subject matter* are advanced in Chapter Twenty-six.) Part of the impact of each work rests in the sensibilities the artist brought to the crosshatching lines. Villon's rationally dynamic strokes imply more about *Renée* (see Figure 22.1) than a mere facial image. Morandi's carefully controlled lines (see Figure 22.2) concentrate on the uncomplicated poetic plastic forms of a still life. Hogarth's conservative crosshatching yields a surprising and somewhat anecdotal *Lord Lovat* (see Figure 22.3) that borders on mimicry. Rembrandt's more fluid lines (see Figure 22.4) convey at once the wisdom, strength, and humility of the aged Jewish patriarch as well as the playful security of a beloved child.

FIGURE 22.1. Jacques Villon (1875–1963, French): *Renée de Trois Quarts* (1911). Drypoint, 21¼″ × 16″. Baltimore Museum of Art.

FIGURE 22.2. Giorgio Morandi (1890–1964, Italian): *Large Still Life with Coffee Pot* (1933). Etching, 9¹⁵⁄₁₆″ × 13¹¹⁄₁₆″. Art Institute of Chicago.

FIGURE 22.3. William Hogarth (1697–1764, English): *Simon Lord Lovat* (1746). Etching, 14¼″ × 10″. Des Moines Art Center.

FIGURE 22.4. Rembrandt Harmensz. van Rijn (1609–1669, Dutch): *Abraham Caressing Isaac* (ca. 1637). Etching, 4⅝″ × 3½″. Des Moines Art Center.

The admonition "Let what you see dictate your stroke" means just that. The subject matter you choose to draw precipitates the way you draw it—the images, the medium, the stroke. If any process becomes more important than what you are trying to show with it, you are trapped in a technique and technique is "planned effects." Being locked into a technique denies the capacity of art to have an internal dynamic that is, finally, unmanaged. But once again, as every exercise in this book intends, technical information needs to be isolated and studied in the early stages of learning to draw.

A darkened room with a spotlight on the still life or model will help but is not necessary. Strong natural light will work very well.

After working through several small gesture sketches, choose the position for the best composition. Lay out the perimeters of the composition and some of the more strategic proportional points of the composition with half-inch lines. Use the vertical and horizontal calculation measurements. Very lightly, let the gestural line characterize the forms in space. Or, once again, use only your hand and forefinger to seek out the *qualities* of the volumes in space. Now, sketch in very lightly the geometric volumes. Viewing the setup at the sides and back to see where masses and volumes begin, end, are supported, or dissolve could help you, as the closer view of drapery may have helped. Gesture and geometry is the scaffold for values.

Values in crosshatching usually are manipulated through density and pressure. Closer, wider lines indicate darker areas, while lines farther apart drawn with less pressure create lighter areas.

With this problem, we have several other factors that will help build values—namely, the colored paper, a white pencil lead, and a black pencil lead.

The middle-tone color of the paper will be the middle value. Pressure on the white pencil combined with the closeness of lines will achieve the highest lights. Pressure on the black pencil along with the compactness of lines will achieve the lowest, deepest darks. Overlap the white pencil strokes with the black pencil strokes in varying degrees and pressure for upper-middle and lower-middle values. Remember, the paper itself is the middle tone.

Crosshatch

How do you want to work the values of the drawing this time? From lights down, from darks up, from the middle-toned paper down to black and up to white? Which way works best for you? Select your own method of establishing values in building the crosshatch drawing, but keep the whole composition in mind.

Seeing patterns in value is a useful tool, but this exercise should carry your work beyond that point. Keep the translation from eye to paper intense enough so that subtleties in values and volumes are not reduced to shallow markings on the paper which the short repetitious lines can easily induce. Look for the general system of values outlined before—the highlights, light tones, middle tones, shadows, core tones, reflected light, and cast shadows. Watch for a value overlapping another value, making a third tone. Seek out the interplay between volumes of forms and refraction of light.

FIGURE 22.5. Theo van Rysselberghe (1862–1962, Belgian): *Marie Sethe at the Piano* (1891). Conte crayon, 12½″ × 14⅛″. Art Institute of Chicago.

FIGURE 22.6. A student drawing using crosshatch. Black and white pencil on construction paper.

FIGURE 22.7. A student drawing using crosshatch. Black and white pencil on construction paper.

As you can observe in Rysselberghe's crosshatch with conte crayon (see Figure 22.5), the drawing is built without contour lines. The crosshatch builds masses. Edges as such are not defined, but suggested. You may well have volumes coming out of the paper, much the way a ship appears in a fog. If the gesture and geometry of the units in space is informative enough, the short intersecting lines of the crosshatch drawing edges could vignette, or fade gradually, off into the paper (see Figures 22.6 and 22.7).

⌈ 23 ⌉

TWO-DAY STUDY
OF LANDSCAPE STRUCTURE

TOOLS
charcoal and charcoal pencil
paper stick
light charcoal paper, or a 2B, 3B, or
  4B pencil on white or off-white
  paper
viewfinder (such as an empty 35mm
  color slide)
landscape

This landscape exercise is designed as a two-day study. The first day is given to composition and to the geometric and gestural reduction with which you worked in the chapters since drapery. On the second day the drawing is completed after you have returned to the place you have been drawing. The second day is given to adding value shapes to the volumes of the first day.

The outdoor space you will be handling in a landscape is quite different than the interior space of still life and model. For one thing, there is much greater distance between you and what you draw, making shapes less obvious. For another, the lighting will change as the clouds alternately block and move out of the sun's rays. Also, atmosphere may become a problem.

But the "back to nature" problem has its advantages too. By this time in your drawing you should have some facility with drawing processes. This problem gives you a chance to realize a fairly substantial piece of work.

Getting out of the studio and working alone is a chance most students enjoy. So finding a farmyard, a country graveyard, a golf course, a private lake, a quarry, an arboretum, a rocky ledge, a city park, or an abandoned coastline are a few of the countless options. This problem is richer in information if you work with a natural landscape rather than with a cityscape.

Find a point of view in a place that is both comfortable and, if possible, sheltered. Inclement weather is always a professional hazard while drawing landscapes.

Using a viewfinder, which can be any small framing device such as an empty 35mm color slide, scan the landscape for a composition. Hold the viewfinder at a bent-arm's length and close one eye while looking through the opening. You will see how the small frame helps isolate a potential composition. Sketch six or seven gesture compositions to adjust to the limitless space of a landscape. After you settle on one portion of the landscape, denote on your paper the horizon line, the perimeters as well as the vertical/horizontal establishing lines and the general vanishing points for depth. Scan the landscape as you work lightly with the gestures of the volumes you see. Now, lightly draw the geometric structural shapes you will be working with: tree trunks as cylinders, hill as half spheres, lakes as ellipses, rocks as rectangles, cubes, polyhedrons, or whatever. Think about the depth those objects occupy as you place the geometric shapes in space. Space here is not only vertical and horizontal, but recedes a great distance.

A problem that crops up with landscape is what to do about the vast repetitions of nature, such as the leaves on trees. To help understand the components of those masses, observe and draw the largest volumes, such as the half sphere for a treetop, first. Then, look for the smaller volumes, the clumps of leaves, and lightly draw the geometric structures of the leaf clusters. Look carefully. Leaf clusters of a

Two-Day Study

silver maple are not the same as needle clusters of a Scotch pine. Throughout the composition, continue reducing the natural shapes to their individual structural geometry. The transposing process should be done with care, since the gesture and geometric shapes becomes the compositional scaffolding (see Figure 23.1).

The second day, return to the same location at the same time and review your geometric shapes. You may want to change a few. Twenty-four hours ago the shapes looked different.

Most of us understand that hills weigh more than treetops. Now, reinforce that fact by drawing value shapes over the hypothetical geo-metric volumes. The "laying on" of lights and darks will finally suggest the more familiar characteristics that make treetops treetops and hills hills.

Work selectively with values. Take note of growth patterns in leaves, limbs, and grass. Stroke on the contrasting values, giving form to the internal support system. Modulate the values as you go or after you

FIGURE 23.1. A student drawing showing the use of values stroked over geometric volumes in a landscape. Charcoal on white drawing paper.

FIGURE 23.2. A student drawing showing the use of values kept as planes. Charcoal on charcoal paper.

FIGURE 23.3. A student drawing showing the use of values stroked over geometric volumes in a landscape. Graphite on white drawing paper.

FIGURE 23.4. Pieter Brueghel the Elder (ca. 1525–1569, Flemish): *Haymaking (July)* (1565). Oils on oak, 46⅟₁₆″ × 63⅜″. National Gallery, Prague.

have laid them all in. But either way, keep an eye on the total composition. You may have to adjust a few of the local values to darker darks or lighter lights to balance the movement within the composition.

All articulation is difficult. It is exacting and inventive. Your creative translation from nature to gesture to geometry to value to realized landscape gives you the advantage of working with a support system, which can yield knowledgeable, competent, and very individual imagery (see Figures 23.2 and 23.3).

Brueghel (see Figure 23.4) treats his landscape as a setting for human activity. Bresdin, on the other hand (see Figure 23.5), uses no figures and, indeed, keeps those viewing his work removed from it; the tangle of reeds, trees, and branches is dense and forbidding.

In Thiebaud's landscape (see Figure 23.6), with its elegant simplicity, the artist uses minimal value contrasts, while in Zimmerman's drawing (see Figure 23.7), despite its small scale the artist suggests the jagged, solid structure of snow-capped mountains with wide contrasts in value.

FIGURE 23.5. Rodolphe Bresdin: *Le Grand Arbre Noir*
(ca. 1860). Ink on tracing paper, 26″ × 18⅛″. Gemeentemuseum, The Hague.

FIGURE 23.6. Wayne Thiebaud (b. 1920, American): *Landscape* (1965). Pencil, 9″ ×
12″. Allan Stone Gallery, New York.

FIGURE 23.7. William Zimmerman (b. 1920, American): *Icy Fingers* (1973). Acrylic, 5″ × 7″.

Part Six

ANALYTICAL TRACINGS, CRITICISM, AND EXPRESSION

24

ANALYTICAL TRACINGS:
MORE ON COMPOSITION

TOOLS
2B and 3B pencils
5 or 6 sheets of tracing paper
colored pencils
ruler
template with circles and ellipses
art book with color reproductions

Tapestries, architecture, landscaping, jewelry, pottery, painting and drawing, films, plays, photography, and dance—all depend heavily on good composition. Some artists who compose in those fields make their decisions about composition in three dimensions. Others compose only two-dimensionally.

This problem is analytical, designed to help you abstract a master artist's composition layer by layer to show why the selected lines and shapes are so important to a total composition.

To benefit most from this problem, find a book with large color reproductions (let us say at least 5″ × 7″ or 7″ × 9″). Select works by established painters, works that have known subjects, such as still lifes, landscapes, or figures (preferably not portraits). Reproductions of paintings from the Gothic, Renaissance, Northern Renaissance, Baroque, Rococo, German Gothic, Pre-Raphaelites, Barbizon, nineteenth-century Classicists and Romanticists, early Impressionists, Pointillists, Expressionists, Hudson River School, the Ash Can School, Pop Art, and New Realism are likely to yield good examples for this problem. Abstract or nonobjective works will prove clumsy.

A unified composition relies on the arrangement of parts or elements to form a unit of spatial organization. The tracing analysis attempts to separate the elements so that four or five compositional components can be viewed in stages or layers. Use one color reproduction of a painting for the whole problem, but use separate sheets of tracing paper for the separate components: the linear, the geometric, the sight line, the value, and the color composition. For each compositional problem, place a separate sheet of tracing paper over the reproduction.

Because art books with good color reproductions are expensive, be wary of pressing too hard and damaging the book. Such damage is easily done, so take care. We will begin our five tracing analyses with *The Descent from the Cross*, ca. 1435, by Rogier van der Weyden (see Plate I).

The first tracing should seek to reduce the whole work to its linear composition. Line here does not mean contour nor gesture in its pure form. Linear composition requires that you see the most basic verticals, horizontals, diagonals, and curved lines that identify the directions and counterdirections of figures, natural forms, man-made objects, mythological, and spiritual images. In this example, a student reduced the most important linear aspects in this painting by abstracting the curve of a head, the direction of an arm, the drape of cloth, the angle of bodies, the horizontals, diagonals, and verticals of the ladder and cross. Her tracing shows that the painting has a rhythmic linear unity of counterforces throughout the whole work (see Figure 24.1).

Linear unity influences eye movement into a drawing or painting and around a center of interest. Linear composition in other reproductions might stress vertical repetitions in nature, such as trees or the legs of a group of quiet cattle or verticals, horizontals, and diagonals

PLATE I. Rogier van der Weyden (ca. 1400–1460, Flemish): *The Descent from the Cross* (ca. 1435). Panel, 7′ 2⅝″ × 8′ 7⅛″. Prado, Madrid.

PLATE II. Color-shapes composition.

PLATE III. Raffaello Sanzio, known as Raphael (1483–1520, Italian): *The Miraculous Draught of Fishes* (1515–1516). Cartoon, gouache on paper, 141″ × 168″. Victoria and Albert Museum, London.

PLATE IV. Albrecht Dürer (1471–1528, German): *Adam and Eve* (1504). Copperplate engraving, 10″ × 7½″. Museum of Fine Arts, Boston.

PLATE V. Peter Paul Rubens (1577–1640, Flemish): *The Defeat of Sennacherib* (1616–1618). Oil on canvas, 3′ 2⅝″ × 4′ ⅜″. Alte Pinakothek, Munich.

PLATE VI. Pierre-Auguste Renoir (1841–1919, French): *Le Moulin de la Galette* (1876). Oil, 51½″ × 69″. Louvre, Paris.

PLATE VII. Pierre-Paul Prud'hon (1758–1823, French): *La Source* (ca. 1801). Black and white chalk, 21³⁄₁₆″ × 15⁵⁄₁₆″. Sterling and Francine Clark Art Institute, Williamstown, Massachusetts.

PLATE VIII. Rembrandt Harmensz. van Rijn (1606–1669, Dutch): *Female Seated and Bending Forward* (1660–1662). India ink and bistre wash, 11¼″ × 6⁵⁄₁₆″. British Museum, London.

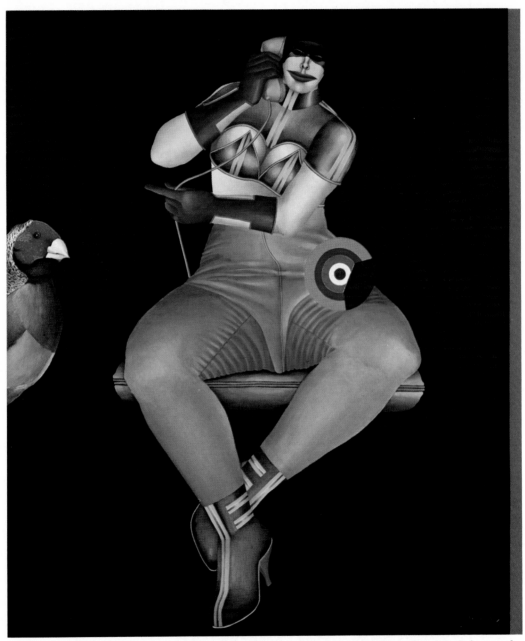

PLATE IX. Richard Lindner (b. 1901, German): *Hello* (1966). Oil on canvas. 70" × 60". Private collection, New York.

PLATE X. Francis Bacon (b. 1910, British): *Head Surrounded by Sides of Beef* (1954). Oil on canvas, 50⅞″ × 48″. Art Institute of Chicago.

PLATE XI. James Ensor (1860–1949, Belgian): *The Artist's Father in Death* (1887). Pencil, black crayon, opaque white on brown paper, 6¾″ × 9″. Private collection.

PLATE XII. James Ensor (1860–1949, Belgian): *The Artist's Father in Death* (1887). Conte crayon. Koninklijk Museum, Antwerp.

FIGURE 24.1. Linear composition.

FIGURE 24.2. Geometric-shapes composition.

of man-made objects such as bridges or buildings. Lines at the edges of dramatic value contrasts, curvilinear lines, and the combinations of lines within figures, clothing, and animals can all serve to sustain a rhythmic balance in a composition.

The second analysis reduces the composition to its geometric volumes. On another sheet of tracing paper placed over the reproduction, isolate objects, natural forms, and people and reduce their masses to the most elementary geometric shapes. Arms and legs will become cylinders or long rectangles, heads turn into circles or elipses, and so on. In the chapter on drapery, you worked with geometric reduction of cloth. Do that as well here with the drapery on the figure. Ships, hills, hats, pillows, and lyre—all can be reduced to a basic geometric shape. Use a ruler if it helps, since the problem is analytical.

You are not, however, just copying existing shapes. You are analyzing and reducing those shapes to their respective geometric equivalents. What you are really looking for are the underlying structures of the volumes used by the artist in creating the illusion of depth (see Figure 24.2).

The illusion of depth, apart from linear perspective, is basically achieved by stroking a selected range of values on paper or canvas. Given the underlying geometric structure first, the values support the visual information established—that is, volume.

Sight Line refers to the direction of the gaze of any persons, birds, animals, or mythological figures in the painting. With that definition, it is obvious that still lifes and landscapes will not involve a sight line.

A straight, but broken line on your next tracing sheet will suggest the sight line. If there are only two or three sight lines involved in the composition, include this analysis with the geometric shapes. But, if there are a number of sight lines, make a separate analysis tracing (see Figure 24.3).

Weak compositions very often are weak because of the interaction of the gaze lines of the people or animals is confused or disoriented so as to send the sight lines off the page, with no apparent focus, compromising the unity of the composition.

The eyes of the two women on the far left and right of the *Descent*

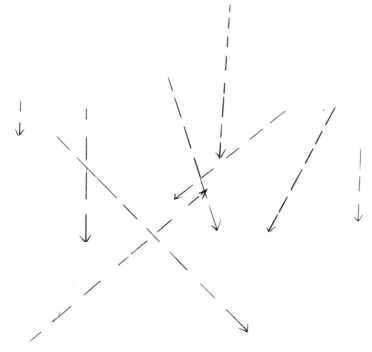

FIGURE 24.3. Sight-lines composition.

FIGURE 24.4. Value-shapes composition.

frame the painting because their bodies are turned toward the center and their gaze is down. The gaze of the man on the ladder pulls us from the truncated overhead space down to the Christ figure, bisecting the composition. Each gaze of the two men on the left looking away from the picture plane intersects with gazes from men on the right. The intersection point of two of those sight lines draws our eye to the stigmata of the Christ. The intersection point of the other two psychological lines draws our eye to the knees of the central figure, Christ. The gaze of the woman above Mary looks down at her, and Mary's eyes, though closed, are facing us squarely. Because the linear flow of arms and drapery is so strong, our eyes follow Mary's arm down to the skull, whose staring sockets take us back to the central figure again. The subtle interlocking system of the sight line with the linear flow draws us into the work and moves us in a cradling rhythm throughout the painting.

The fourth analytical problem concerns value shapes and is worked out on still another sheet of tracing paper. By now you should understand that what you must see are value shapes and not objects colored in. The red of a garment may well be, in grays, the same value as the blue of a drape just behind the garment, making that whole shape of both drape and garment one middle-tone gray. Work your way across the composition in values using a 2B and a 3B pencil (see Figure 24.4).

Value can be used to create the illusion of depth. Value shapes can be seen as pattern. Uniting patterns of values as they are used to achieve spatial depth is to understand the subtle play of lights and darks and artist uses to sustain movement within the composition.

The last compositional analysis, color shapes, is done with colored pencils. The shapes to isolate are the shapes of areas most closely associated with each other in color. If the shape of a shawl, cowel, face, and background are all yellow-gold, these shapes should be combined to become one large yellow-gold shape.

Reduce the colors of the painting reproduction to the five or six most obvious colors. Use the colored pencils that are closest to them in hue (color). If you use more than six colors, you will work too long on the problem and lose sight of the information being sought, i.e., what the general color composition of this artist is. This problem lets you see the dispersed patterns of specific colors throughout an artist's composition.

Draw the color shapes in, using a fairly steady, heavy pressure to insure consistent color with the pencils (see Plate II).

A good test for accuracy in your tracing analyses can be had by holding the value tracing over the color tracing against a light. How close is the combination to the reproduction you have just analyzed?

By isolating individual elements of composition through use of a major artist's painting in reproduction, you will begin to appropriate thinking processes for approaching your own drawing, for establishing point of view, composition, underlying structures, and, finally, values and colors.

25

RESPONSIVE ANALYSIS:
A CRITICAL METHOD

Tools
art museum
notebook
pencil

For better or worse, most of us like what we are told to like. When those we regard as informed and respected enjoy something, we probably adjust our enjoyment accordingly. The problem, of course, is that we may claim pleasures we do not truly understand. What we need, therefore, is an emotional honesty and what might be called a critical methodology. Since neither will function without practice, the improvements good criticism can affect is not at this point premature. Candor, of course, is something this book can only encourage, not exercise. But, chances are that as your judgments become increasingly analytical, your pleasures will find independent security.

Certainly your drawing should improve. Through intelligent criticism you will learn to accomplish some of the thinking about space and illusion that experienced artists have successfully managed ahead of you. You will see your own work in a context, recognizing both its uniqueness and its generality.

Responsive Analysis

The critical methodology advanced in this chapter is built on four premises: honesty, description, interpretation, judgment. At this point, the student's task brings sensory responses and intellectual responses into a working relationship: each tests the other and, at the same time, derives a legitimate interpretation of a painting or drawing.

Two tips for beginning critics: work from comparative standpoints, and, as exercises, select works with identifiable subject matter.

Honesty. Look at the work. What is the impact of the whole? What emotions are triggered?

Description. Let the work stand for itself, independent of your feelings. Describe the images in detail, but avoid value-laden adjectives. Describe the mode of representation, tectonic or theatrical. (These contrasting modes will be discussed later in this chapter). Some of what you describe about the images and the modes may be expanded in the next step as you interpret the influence of one on the other.

Interpretation. Interpret the materials, the formal elements, the mode, and the image as they shape the subject in the work. Your ordering and assessment of those clues in material, element, image, and mode contribute to the subject and should lead you to articulate the affective statement in the work. What Gestalt or wholeness is the work showing us?

Judgment. In so far as you have decided what the work shows, was it successful? Does your judgment on the work's success connect with what happened to you in the first step?

Here is a brief glossary of the formal elements:

line: any discrete marking stroke that is vertical, horizontal, diagonal, curvilinear.

color: the individual hues and their intensities, brightness/dullness.

value: lights and darks.

texture: the material surface of things.

perspective (at least three ways of achieving the appearance of depth):

1. linear perspective—the use of vanishing points and converging lines.

2. aerial perspective—the diffusion of colors, values, and textures from foreground to background.

3. overlapping shapes

point of view: the station point of the artist, or where the artist places the viewer.

sight line: the direction of a gaze.

composition: integrated affective spatial organization, which includes the materials, the elements, the mode, and the images.

The formal elements are rarely incorporated with equal stress in all works. In criticism, select the most important elements you see, and discuss those. For instance, some artists use only large value shapes and little or no line. Some use vibrant, very intense color shapes; others use pastels. A seated nude first done in cool, pastel colors such as blues and grays and then drawn in garish-colored inks, would, in comparison, reveal marked contrast of association and symbol.

From the method and arrangement of colors, lines, values, and shapes, images emerge. Signals within a drawing or painting make us notice the subject, which is larger than any one image. But what signals within the materials, the mode, the images, and formal elements lead us to understand the significant idea, the affective statement, embodied in the subject?

A word here about signals. A subject signal is anything about the image that informs the viewer about the subject. The image of a figure on a horse coming toward us, moving away from us, or walking parallel to our picture plane embodies different meanings within a drawing or painting. A nude figure lying down, standing up, or lounging against an object prompts alternative meaning. But the image has to be united with the way it is presented to be an informative signal for the subject. Once again, clues from the materials, the formal elements, the image and the mode of presentation brought to bear on the subject communicate the affective statement, or the significant idea, in a work of art. What is being shown? What is the meaning embodied in the subject?

The critical methodology previously outlined will be helpful to you in analyzing most drawings or paintings with representational images. Before we begin, however, a brief but important analytical aid will be discussed.

Heinrich Wölfflin, in his *Principles of Art History,* set out to classify the sweeping stylistic changes in art between the sixteenth and seventeenth centuries. Wölfflin dwelt on the methods used to represent images. In identifying methods, he articulated concepts corresponding to the two major modes in representational art that continued from the Renaissance through the seventeenth century. He identified those modes as imitation and decoration. A more useful terminology might be the *tectonic* and the *theatrical modes,* and these terms seem applicable for representational art into the twentieth century. The tectonic mode shows unified formal clarity, while the theatrical mode shows unified indeterminate clarity.

The two concepts are set forth to help you think in a comparative framework. Tectonic and theatrical describe extremes, neither of which exists very often in a pure form in recent centuries. Hopefully, you will view them as tendencies in the art works you analyze. Understanding the two systems will give you a more effective basis for selecting the structural clues (actually, morphological clues) that weigh so heavily in the meaning of a work of art.

The illustrations selected are fairly pure examples of the two modes. They will not be discussed, but are visual references for you as you practice applying the tectonic (see Plates III and IV) and the theatrical modes (see Plates V and VI).

The Tectonic Mode	The Theatrical Mode
1. Line (Contour)	*1. Gesture and Mass*
Line sets the boundaries of things. Beauty of the full form is shown in the sensitive outline. Line is superior to any other element such as color or value. Line yeilds security. Line gives uniform information as the eye moves from part to separate part.	Gesture and mass dispense with line. Boundaries are not stressed. Value supports movement and impression, not geometric volume. The whole picture is seen, not its parts.
2. Plane	*2. Recession (Depth)*
The measure of depth is described as a vertical and horizontal compactness. Volumes are placed close to and parallel to the picture plane. Little recession is felt even though linear perspective has been used.	Depth is the impression of sweeping into space by way of diagonals or spirals, lights and darks. Figures are placed farther back of and sometimes obliquely to the picture plane.
3. Closed Composition	*3. Open Composition*
The composition contains a stable equilibrium. The placement of the formal elements produces no tension, but perfect harmony. Every direction has its counterforce. The composition is self-contained and "pointing everywhere back to itself." [1]	The open composition presents a looser sense of order, resulting in tension, not satisfaction. Diagonals rupture the tectonic stability of verticals and horizontals. The open composition conceals its structure to promote what Wölfflin calls an "oscillating balance." The purpose of an open composition is to appear limitless.

4. Unified Parts

Separate parts maintain independence though qualified by the whole. The whole is unified in the "harmony of free parts." [2]

4. Unified Whole

One single theme predominates over all parts. The parts relinquish uniformity and independence to movement and depth.

5. Absolute Clarity

Declarative, lucid, objective revelation of the forms allows the spectator to apprehend each part. Uniform emphasis prompts contemplation.

6. Relative Clarity

Objective clarity is avoided, which invites supposition. Clarity in color, forms, and values are subsidiary to the indeterminate impressions.

Assuming that the tectonic and the theatrical modes are clarified to some degree, let us begin our criticism with the four major steps here recapitulated.

Honesty
(Step One)

What is the impact of the whole? What emotions are triggered?

Description
(Step Two)

Describe the images in detail, as they are. Describe the mode tendency in the work. Is it tectonic, theatrical, or some of both?

Interpretation
(Step Three)

What is the affective statement? Interpret the materials, the formal elements, the images, and the modal presentation insofar as they contribute to the subject and afford meaning.

Judgment
(Step Four)

According to your decisions in step three, was the work successful? Does your judgment here coincide with your original response?

For the first analysis, we will compare two drawings with similar subjects: Pierre-Paul Prud'hon's black and white chalk drawing *La Source* (see Plate VII), and Rembrandt van Rijn's drawing in India ink and bistre wash *Female Nude Seated and Bending Forward* (see Plate VIII).

PRUD'HON'S LA SOURCE

Step One: General reactions are "It's beautiful and delicate." "Makes me feel cold and removed." "The woman is not real." My reaction: "It is quiet and pleasurable, an archetype, an ideal woman."

Step Two: A nude female is seated on a cloth which covers a stone structure. Her legs are crossed at the ankles. She is looking down to her upturned left palm, held to her side. Her right elbow rests on her right thigh as she touches her right fingers to the side of her face. She wears a band in her hair.

To her right there is a stream of water issuing from a rock and spilling into a small basin just below.

The light comes from above and in front of the figure.

Outlines are obvious. The L-shaped composition is planar with dominant verticals and horizontals. The figure is close to and parallel to the picture plane. The composition is very stable. All parts are treated with equal importance, and everything is clearly defined. The work is strongly tectonic in structure.

Step Three: Prud'hon chose to work in black and white chalk on blue paper. He worked in short diagonal strokes then modeled gently to achieve the soft lighting effects on the body, making edges pronounced. The colors, medium, and approach support the impression that the woman is idealized and removed from an everyday existence.

Her contemplative body attitude keeps our eyes in a diamond-shaped motion beginning with her feet, moving up the diagonal to the knee, to the elbow, now to the diagonal of her right arm, and then to the soft, round head. Her central sight line as well as her lax arm draws us down to the hand. The fingers gently point to the left thigh and so, back to her feet, completing the geometric diamond parallelogram movement, contained within itself.

That diamond-shaped figure is stabilized by the very sturdy vertical and horizontal planes of the L-shaped rock and by the fact that she is seated. She is parallel and close to our picture plane. Our point of view places us seated at her feet, our eyes at the level of her stomach looking up a little at her. Because of her proximity to our picture plane and our seated point of view, we are paradoxically with her, yet removed.

The flow of the drapery, the angle of the legs and foot move our eyes horizontally to "The Source," this being a reference to "woman," implying she is the source or wellspring of life. This woman is nude rather than naked. She is youthful, fair, and virginal; an elevated, removed symbol of ideal woman.

Step Four: Prud'hon drew a neoclassical nude imbued with what is "fair and forever" in woman. While the technical skill is impressive, the image presented seems sentimental now because "ideal figures" tend to prompt periodic veneration. Historically placed, the drawing may have affected more pleasure than a contemporary viewer is willing to feel. However, the subject presented, "Woman, the Source," speaks to the "universal feminine," which is both historic and immediate. My judgment of this work supports the emotional reaction in Step One.

REMBRANDT'S FEMALE NUDE SEATED AND BENDING FORWARD

In Rembrandt's drawing, also a nude female, the artist utilizes the elements common to Prud'hon's drawing but employs them differently, using another medium, ink and bistre. Let us apply the same steps of criticism to the Rembrandt.

Step One: General student reactions: "It's beautiful, I love it." "Nice and earthy, I get good feelings." "It's simple but dynamic." My reaction: "It is an ordinary woman, uncomplicated, beautiful. The impact of the drawing is startling in its immediacy, and it is delightful."

Step Two: This is a drawing of a nude female seated on what appears to be a bookcase. Her right heel is slightly elevated resting on one of the books on the floor. She is bending forward reaching toward her left ankle, looking in the same direction. The lighting is a little above head level, front and right a little of the figure. She has a band around her hair.

Gesture is stressed in this drawing. There is some depth, but not much. The composition is loosely structured. The theme is more important than the individual parts. Clarity rests in the immediate impact of the work. The mode is more theatrical than tectonic.

Step Three: The predominant line in this drawing is a vertical brush stroke on the left, wide enough to become a shape, thereby dissolving line as line. The figure emerges from the rest of the dark, bold brushwork because of the contrast of lights against darks. The woman's cast shadow shape helps to identify her positive shape.

The medium itself, ink wash and bistre, and the color, earth tones, lend credence to the informality of the woman and her pose. This would suggest she is an individual and human.

Lighting on the figure does not come from a holy or mythical source. It is bright, natural lighting from a window or perhaps a lamp within the room. The light seems direct and fairly intense in that the value shapes are dramatic, high intensities against low intensities. There are few middle tones.

The attitude of the woman, leaning forward, gives less a feeling of instability than a feeling of "the moment caught." There is an immediacy about this drawing that is not in Prud'hon's work. Both Prud'hon and Rembrandt have used an L-shaped composition into which they have placed a nude in a contrapuntal theme of diagonals. Because of the diagonals of arms, legs, and the sight line of the figure, the rhythm established in both drawings sustains a continuous motion within the center of interest. But Rembrandt's composition feels open.

Rembrandt's nude is less refined and older; she looks as if she's about to scratch an ankle in an everyday, mundane gesture.

While there are similarities in the Prud'hon pose and the Rembrandt pose—both are nude females looking down to the left, and seated in a simple setting—the implications are quite different. Rembrandt's is a drawing of a nude individual woman out of everyday life, not a symbol of woman as in Prud'hon's.

Step Four: Rembrandt's image of a woman manages a simple and unostentatious statement of an everyday act. The subject presented, the "Individual Woman," evokes memories of the mundane action which prompts us to acknowledge the individual but does not move us to reflect on an ideal. Our first reactions of step one have been sustained throughout this analysis.

For the second analysis, we will compare two paintings with dissimilar subjects: Richard Lindner's *Hello,* an oil painting dated 1966 (see Plate IX) with Francis Bacon's *Head Surrounded by Sides of Beef,* an oil painting of 1954 (see Plate X).

LINDNER'S HELLO

Step One: General student reactions: "It makes me feel sad." "I feel sorry for her." "I couldn't live with that." My reaction: "That painting is sardonic, and I feel wryly displeased."

Step Two: A woman dressed in a satinlike purple, blue, and gold uniform is seated on a cushion, face front, holding a phone to her head in her right hand. The space where she is seated is not identifiable. While holding the phone cord in her left hand, the woman seems to be pointing to a bird, a parrot, only partially shown on the left of the painting. There is a target on the woman's left hip and thigh. The woman's eyes are covered with something resembling a mask.

Line predominates, giving uniform information as our eye moves from part to part. Space is planar, vertical, and horizontal. The stable symmetry of the woman seated on the horizontal green cushion is disrupted by the strong diagonals of the arms and legs. The figure is extraordinarily close to and parallel to our picture plane. The composition points everywhere back to itself. Parts are related to the whole, but remain independent. Clarity rests in every area except the eyes. This painting emphasizes the tectonic mode even though the image is flamboyant.

Step Three: The colors Lindner uses are surprisingly dramatic, made so by the starkness of the black background, an identifiable space. The clothes of the woman, because of the intense colors, satin tectures, and costume style, suggest a type of uniform, indicating sameness in sleazy conformity.

Diminution of the woman's head in relation to the enlarged mass of hips and thighs suggests women are good for things other than contemplative thought. This suggestion is sustained through the enlarged mouth, the covered eyes, the "parroting" on the phone.

While the dramatic diagonals of the legs and thighs bring us into the work, we are held within the composition through the repetitive, but smaller diagonals of the stripes on her jacket and boots and the diagonal value-contrast shapes of her arms.

The shape of the bird's beak is repeated in the V shape of the pants seams as well as in the triangular shapes of the bra, supporting the cyclical visual rhythm already established by the diagonals. (The figure of a bird in art history usually symbolizes the phallus.[3] That significance may be useful here because of our point of view, and just to the right of the woman's crotch is a target, a "redesigned" parrot's head and eye.) The direction of the finger pointing to the bird is countered by the sight line of the parrot's eyes back to the woman.

Linear perspective, barely visible here in the recession of the figure, knee to backbone, establishes a limited depth. The suggested recession of the pillow coupled with the lines of the thighs moves us again to the center of interest.

There is an unstable quality to the composition, a diamond shape on its point, in spite of the strong green horizontal of the pillow. Instability is promoted by the lack of information about the cushion. Natural space as we understand it is not depicted here. Lindner's space is unreal, lending credence to the idea that this is a stylization of a female figure.

Step Four: Because the figure is without individuality, the image can be viewed as a symbolic statement of one kind of woman. A dramatic statement, and perhaps degrading as a standard, it nevertheless helps the painting establish its dehumanized view clearly. The idea presented once again cycles back to our original reactions.

BACON'S HEAD SURROUNDED BY SIDES OF BEEF

Bacon's painting uses a different subject but similar colors.

Step One: General reactions: "I'm repelled." "He's screaming. It makes me nervous." "Who wants raw meat hanging around? It is repulsive." My reaction: "Another comment on desperation. Makes me feel anguished."

Step Two: A man appears to be seated, his mouth open. He wears both something on his head and a robe of some kind. Sides of meat hang on either side of the man, just behind him. The beef, man, and chair are set within one small area of enclosed space. An arrow on the left points down to the man.

Gestural strokes imply mass in most areas in this painting. The cube or box is the only structure, if it is a structure, that is bounded by line. There is little depth implied. The figure and sides of beef face us, close to the picture plane, giving a tectonic structure to the visual space. But the indefinite spatial orientation, the predominating theme, and the lack of clarity make this work more theatrical than tectonic.

Step Three: We are brought into this painting through the use of diagonals (the lower right and upper left white lines against the black background, as well as through the carcass legs), all of which stop abruptly at the smeared shape of a screaming face, white, stark against the dark colors around the face.

The hat, the clothes, the chair could be judicial or religious because the shapes and colors indicate clerical or legal garb.

The boxed, enclosed space is dark, with illumination coming from an unknown source, sustaining the anxiety already established by the scream and raw meat.

If one looks carefully, directly above and behind the man's head, there are two childlike profiles in the splayed beef, all the more dramatic because of the starkness of the values employed. Going even further, the hind legs of the carcasses could be shrouds hovering over those skeletal profiles, even while extending down the sides. The amputated forelegs of the carcasses go through the man's figure, ending subtly, but abruptly, in the shapes of clenched fists. The carcasses now seem to be enveloping the man; ghostly, everpresent specters permeating the seated figure.

Linear perspective is used in a limited way to shape the enclosed space and, with the white horizontal lines, helps to stabilize the composition, even though the darkness is not identifiable.

Our point of view is above the man, looking down on him, giving the viewer a superior position. And, abruptly, the black arrow pointing down toward the man appears almost as if placed on a glass plane separated from the rest of the painting. The arrow, by its placement and direction, seems accusatory.

Step Four: Bacon painted this in the early 1950s, after the Second World War, so the image shown would seem to be a scathing comment on the impotence of judicial and religious figures during the slaughter of the Jews. Viewed ahistorically, the painting betrays an inner anguish or guilt felt by an authority unable to act, only scream, during carnage going on nearby.

Each of these paintings presents a different idea while using similar colors, and each of these paintings effects uneasy emotional responses. These two factors seem to be the only similarities. The images certainly are not similar. The comparison exemplifies that through the arrangement of like colors and values, an image emerges; but subject signals, modal presentation, and the arrangement of the formal elements point us to quite disparate ideas in the two works.

Most of the information you derive from a painting or drawing has to be deduced from what is given in the work. Indeed, this is always the primary information. If you desire more, however, check titles, dates, read catalogues, or review the appropriate books. Placing a work in its historical context may add new dimensions to the presented "idea."

There are some pitfalls to avoid.

Telling stories is one of them. Associative values are necessary in good criticism to denote the "idea" in a work of art, but they do not serve you well if you use them to construct narratives. A young man and woman seen looking in opposite directions does not necessarily mean the couple cannot stand each other and want to flee. If a work of art strikes a responsive chord in you, it is evoking a memory of something you have already experienced. But one can easily become sentimental and invent irrelevant stories about scenes, people, or actions depicted in a work.

Stressing only the formal problems gives an analysis simply of the structures in the painting. It is limited because one finds no meaning in the work. If the work *is* meaningless, find the structural failing that denotes this.

Discussing only the images and your response to them is not a sensible course either. If the student misses the reasons for the affective statement, he betrays a visual illiteracy, a failure to reason through association. The elements you choose to discuss may not be those intended by the artist, but analyzing the elements, the structural clues, and the subject signals you do choose is a surer key to the worth of the work than talking about the pleasure or moral indignation the work prompts from you.

Avoid analyzing the artist. A person is in a museum, gallery, or art center to comprehend the work, not the person producing it. Try to reach for the affective statement in the works. Leave psychoanalysis to professionals in the privacy of their offices.

Now, your assignment: go to a museum and analyze originals.

26

EXPRESSION

A chapter on expression is almost premature in a beginning study of drawing. But many students insist on bringing it up. Sooner or later the questions are asked: "Is what I'm doing art?" "Is my style obvious?" "Am I expressing anything distinctive in my work?" Concern about expression is understandable even though the topic is complex. The long history of standards and tastes and the many theories of pleasure and beauty cannot be neatly summarized in a few paragraphs. All this chapter offers is an outline of premises that try to distinguish between what an artist does and what his or her produced work shows.

The student should be alerted to a basic problem. Susanne Langer has observed that traditional aesthetics are beset with logical difficulties "aggravated by the fact that there are two opposite perspectives from which every work of art may be viewed: that of its author and that of its spectators." [1] These two perspectives have been an assumption throughout this book, especially through the chapter on criticism. Rather than attempting to settle the philosophic difficulties, this chapter asserts simply that a beginning student will profit from recognizing the distinctions. You should know the difference between *expressive content*, what the artist supplies, and *affective statement*, what the work supplies.

What the artist does first of all is make choices, both rationally and intuitively. The artist proceeds from an intention, an *idea*, within

Expression

which qualities, attributes, and relationships inhere. At first, the idea may be nothing more than an intention, the initial stroke on a piece of paper. Or the idea may be a complete preconception. Any decisions used to represent the idea will supply its *form*, which is what makes an artist's idea knowable to others and often to himself or herself. Form is constituted of the physical shape, scale, and material as well as integrative tension and resolution. But what is integrated and re-solved is your *subject*. Some words in this paragraph need a certain amount of definition.

The *subject* is the "something" that is drawn or painted. It resides within your paper or canvas. It is usually comprised of many images but signifies more than the sum of those images. (*Subject matter* is the conventional way of referring to things "out there," such as a model, a still life, a landscape, a memory, an invention.)

Shape relates to the design of the physical support the artist selects, and includes the *materials* from which the form will be realized. *Scale* is size. *Integrative tension* denotes the ordering of the formal elements of composition, modal presentation, and the image the artist uses to unify and clarify the idea. And *resolution* means that the expression seems complete, the work is finished.

An identifiable interdependence of form and idea is unique to each artist—that is, his or her *style*. Style is inherent in each person. Just as fingerprints are similar but distinctive, so is the stroke, the vision, the taste of each person who attempts to draw. Style should never be fabricated. Insofar as style can be acquired, it unfolds from repeated choice-making. Looking, thinking, choosing, drawing, practicing, and practicing again—these are the words attached to a personalized competence.

You will draw or paint *what* you have to, the *way* you want to. Whether what you complete is a work of art is a concern relative to the work itself, not to what you claim for it. The work will present itself independently to all of its viewers (including its creator), to per-sons who may or may not see that the resolutions embody a significant idea and form.

In short, what you provide is competence. The work you produce competently provides art. The viewer should experience your work as a whole first. An intuitive response takes place. From that intuitive event emerges meaning. At this stage, idea and form gradually become analytical tools for the observer. But, rather than treating idea and form as categories of choice, they now become components for evaluation. *Idea* now consists of those clues or signals (in image, method, and formal elements) that inform us, that prompt an attitude, that connect us to universals, and that let us know the emotional weight of what is presented. *Form* is comprised of the factors that exhibit visual organization (composition) and denote wholeness (unity of materials with idea). Together, idea and form communicate an affective statement, which is what moves us, what commands our thought, and is, finally, what determines the capacity of a work to be considered art.

Comparing Rodolphe Bresdin's *The Flight into Egypt* (see Figure 26.1) with Giovanni Domenico Tiepolo's *The Holy Family Passing under an Arch* (see Figure 26.2), we find that each is a work of art for different reasons.

FIGURE 26.1. Rodolphe Bresdin: *The Flight into Egypt* (1855). Lithograph, 22¼″ × 17½″.

FIGURE 26.2. Giovanni Domenico Tiepolo (1727–1804, Italian): *The Holy Family Passing under an Arch* (ca. 1750–1755). Etching, 7¼″ × 9⅝″. Private collection.

Bresdin's lithograph keeps us removed yet interested. We are observing a unique threesome (all three have haloes) sitting beyond us by a stream in a landscape full of dense, tangled, gnarled trees. The generally threatical mode supports a dramatic moment in the life of this family. Because of the isolation of the oddly lit otherworldly figures, we feel we are witnessing an unusual event, a select family pausing in their flight from grave danger.

Tiepolo's etching, on the other hand, lets us join the crowd watching the family leave. Nothing implies fear. The tectonic mode implies stability. The daylight, the open space, and the position, kinds, and attitudes of all the figures lead us to feel that the three are on a long journey. An enigmatic halo shape above the head of Mary is the barest suggestion that this woman is unique. Because of that, and because they are set apart from the small crowd, the family remains very simply, special.

Form and idea are unified in these works. These prints signify wholly articulated symbols. Each work retains a sphere of illusion. Each has images abstracted, modified, and arranged. And each presents insights to living experience.

However, one of James Ensor's studies of *The Artist's Father in Death* seems more persuasive than the other. The study using opaque white on brown paper (see Plate XI) seems a consummate picture of death—translucent skin, paleness—timelessness, the soul's cold container. But the second illustration, in comparison, seems less convincing (see Plate XII). The dynamics of the conte crayon strokes above the figure effect a turbulent atmosphere in contrast to the picture of death, an old man's quiet expiration on a pillow.

An affective difficulty might rest with integrative tension as well as with materials. The heavy, black crayon strokes do not seem to clarify this man's death. Those same strokes might work in describing a more anguished from of dying. But for the father on his deathbed, the dense, diagonal strokes prompt some confusion between idea and form.

If you are a student who is not especially concerned to move your drawing toward a fine art, this discussion of expression may seem irrelevant. Perhaps you are learning to draw as a service to another special interest, a different kind of visualizing such as scene design, weaving, medical illustration, or other fields using visual communication. No problems; for you, drawing is a tool. Your expressive needs will be supported by drawing but must be resolved in other media. However, if you are among those who want to enter critical arenas of drawing with your own expressive content, a few warnings might save grief.

1. Knowledgeable persons may well reject your work. Equally unsettling, however, is premature acceptance. Try not to stumble into experiences of censure or commendation (in art shows or with galleries) until you are equipped with secure critical faculties of your own. If you can't see the strengths and weaknesses in your own work, chances are you will misconstrue signals you receive from others.

2. Before you make any claim for producing Art, capital *A,* get yourself well in touch with the major traditions, theories, and examples

Expression

contained in five thousand years of art history. Remember, each time
you refine a pencil stroke, you are keeping company with many before
you. A serious artist knows something of his or her heritage.

3. The power of your drawing rests in the work, not in your feelings
about the work. Sincerity is not enough. Neither is emoting, although
sometimes the line between self-expression and therapy is a fine one.
This does not mean that you should avoid subject matter that has
charged emotional meaning—far from it. Feelings are as much a
raw material as your pencil or charcoal. But feelings are meaningless
without a competent form/idea embodiment.

So, when you ask, "How can I know what I am doing is Art?" the
most serviceable response is that a great deal of technical discipline
usually comes before much creativity. Once a lucid understanding of
drawing has been grasped, peculiar spatial difficulties will arise as if on
cue. Your solutions become your style. And that is what this book is
all about.

Part Seven

SOME
EXPERIMENTATION

⌐27⌐

REPETITION OF IMAGES

Tools
*charcoal paper, middle
  tone to light tone
charcoal pencil
paper stick*

Experimentation is a very necessary part of any art form. Each of us seeks ways to express ourselves. But the difference between a doodle on a pad of paper and a doodle in the Louvre hangs on its expressive form and, probably, meaning.

Experimentation is a way to test what you know against what you want to know. You need to know the potentialities of various materials—pencils, chalks, charcoals, ink, paints, brushes, pens, papers. You can test different modes or processes using line, value, color, texture, perspective, and composition. You can experiment with images, either representational or nonrepresentational. And somewhere in the continued process of drawing, your distinctive perception will find its own order out of myriad possibilities.

This chapter and the following two suggest some exercises in experimentation: repetitions of like shapes, drawing dissimilar and unrelated shapes, then collage and mixed media. Chapter Thirty offers abbreviated alternatives to problems you have already solved. The exercises certainly do not exhaust experimental possibilities. They are intended as a springboard for your own curiosity and discipline in drawing.

Repetition of images is designed to offer initial experiences in creating a composition through the repeated use of one shape.

Ruscha and Price have repeated the fly in an assortment of sizes (see Figure 27.1). The disbelief of the frog at his luck is obvious as he turns to the viewer.

Magritte, in his consistently enigmatic way, repeats his own image twice, seen from behind (see Figure 27.2). One silhouettes nighttime, one silhouettes daytime. A curious perspective juxtaposes the two human images housing deep space and places them next to vertical wood wall paneling. His drawing is a mysterious ordering of visible things.

The images you choose can be repeated vertically, horizontally, or diagonally within the same composition. The size of the image can be

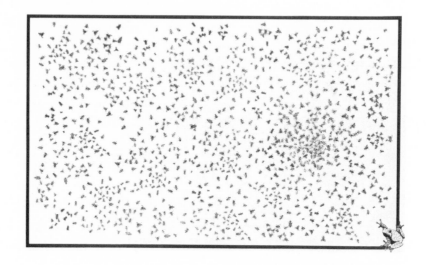

FIGURE 27.1. Ed Ruscha (b. 1937, American) and Kenneth Price (b. 1935, American): *Frog and Flies* (1969). Color lithograph, 34″ × 23⅛″. Des Moines Art Center.

FIGURE 27.2. René Magritte (1898–1967, Belgian): *The Thought Which Sees* (1965). Graphite, 15¾″ × 11⅝″. Museum of Modern Art, New York.

superlife-sized, life-sized, diminished, miniature, or combinations of sizes. The drawing can be worked either as flat shapes of value or as modulating values.

Whichever option is chosen, one object or one object and its cast shadow will be the subject matter. The heavy cast-iron stand of a drawing table lends itself well to repetitions. Letting the stand and its shadow appear to recede by making each image smaller, repeating the image in a circular motion, drawing the stand and its shadow repeatedly vertically, which makes a horizontal movement across the page, are a few of the alternatives to consider.

Choose some item, and place it on a table or a floor (shiny, reflective surfaces are good for this exercise). Shine a light on the object if you need to, until you have what you want in value shapes with both the object and its cast shadow.

A gesture sketch of this problem is quite important. You are designing a composition in stages. The gesture sketch not only will help identify the best perspective, but will show you what happens when you change the scale of one of the repeated images. Finally, the gesture sketch will allow you to see the possibilities of the whole composition.

Lay out the perimeters and establishing lines of the first image and

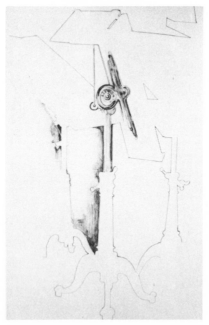

FIGURE 27.4. Student drawing using repetition of images. Charcoal and chalk on charcoal paper.

FIGURE 27.3. Student drawing using repetition of images. Graphite on white drawing paper.

FIGURE 27.5. Student drawing using repetition of images. Ink on white drawing paper.

Repetition of Images

shadow with the half-inch lines. Lightly draw the gesture and geometry of the volumes. What is the next repetition? An enlarged image? A miniature image? Where will you place it? Lay out the perimeters and establishing half-inch lines of the second, repeated image. Lightly draw the gesture and geometry of the volumes. Do the same thing with the third. If using a fourth and fifth image seems feasible, place those compositional establishing lines into the total composition as well.

The whole composition of repeated images should be completely thought out before completing the drawing. If the whole composition is not adequately planned out, the drawing can appear to be running off the page. Investing hours in the values in one area, only to find your next repeated value shapes too clumsy to use again in the composition is far too time consuming and frustrating, so don't risk it. Work through the gesture and geometry of each section of the repetition until the composition works as a whole. Then work in values (see Figures 27.3, 27.4, and 27.5).

⌐28⌐

SELECTED COMPOSING

Tools
2B or 3B pencil
several 5″ × 7″ sheets of newsprint
light charcoal paper
charcoal pencils
paper stick
a room full of things

Select isolated and unrelated objects such as a skate, a wine bottle, a potato masher, a book, a doll's head, a reflection, or a shadow, and you have a new way to create a composition. This time, the objects you work with will not be grouped together as a still life. The end result may or may not look like a still life. The dissimilarity of the shapes you select—whether negative or positive, light or dark—reaffirms, as each new shape is added, the importance of choosing selectively to unify space. Choice and selectivity, unity, balance, dramatic focus, organized space—all represent human artistic judgments and do not exist in nature as such. For instance, in a composition of apparently unrelated shapes, you will inevitably need to resolve the "background" uncertainty. In relation to "what" do the individual shapes exist?

With your eyes, scan a room, selecting the shapes most interesting to you. Study the positives and negatives of objects, their reflections and shadows, just as you find them. Now create your composition on paper as you walk around the room, drawing in gesture on a 5″ × 7″ sheet of newsprint. Move quickly and easily to another position for another shape. Experiment with the space and the shapes. It is soon clear that not all things need to be drawn as the law of gravity dictates. On the paper, turn some shapes upside down or sideways if that repositioning will help the total composition. Do several quick but resolved gesture compositional studies on separate sheets and then select the strongest composition with which to work.

With that composition in mind, draw a five- or ten-minute study of the value shapes on a fresh 5″ × 7″ sheet of newsprint. See if those value shapes work as well for the same composition as the gesture did. Modulate some areas and leave others flat, but experiment with the continuous formation of shapes or what might be called the push-pull plasticity of modeling. If the values can stand alone as a strong composition (just as the gesture composition stood alone), move to the charcoal paper.

Lay in the half-inch perimeter and establishing lines of the composition; lightly draw the gestures of the volumes and the geometric structures; then work in values.

Should your 5″ × 7″ value-study composition "fall apart" visually, see what you can do to correct it. Use another reflection, shadow, or shape. Stand or sit at a different angle to one or more of the items you have drawn until you create a resolved composition of unlike things and shapes.

The drawing should not be a composition of isolated drawn objects colored in. Ideally, it has emerged as a drawing showing versatile use of the art elements merging into your own combination—both definitive and unified.

Your artistic stamp should be on this drawing. You will see what no one else will see (see Figures 28.1 and 28.2).

FIGURE 28.1. Student composition of selected shapes and objects. Charcoal on charcoal paper.

FIGURE 28.2. Student composition of selected shapes and objects. Charcoal on charcoal paper.

$\lceil 29 \rceil$

COLLAGE AND MIXED MEDIA

TOOLS
white drawing paper
newspaper or a brown paper bag
glue
pencils, charcoal, ink, chalk,
   carbon pencils (any medium
   used to date in the course)
still life or model

We have reached a good place in our exercises to incorporate insights from a fairly recent turning point in the history of art. Heretofore, we have thought of space in Renaissance terms. Linear perspective achieved for us an illusion of depth from a fixed field of vision seen through and established on an imagined picture plane, usually rectangular.

What happens when we do not have a fixed field of vision, when we can see all sides of an object simultaneously? Because the eye focuses on only one place at a time, an image drawn with a simultaneous multi-view fractures the object like a field of broken mirrors. Overlapping voids and solids suddenly look like cubes and planes. A new geometry transforms natural appearances into an abstract order which rests in a special space: a vertical, sculptural, bas-relieflike façade.

While the image in Picasso's work (see Figure 29.1) does not portray

FIGURE 29.1. Pablo Picasso (1881–1973, Spanish): *Ambroise Vollard* (1909–1910). Oil on canvas, 36″ × 26½″. Pushkin Museum, Moscow.

nature, nor is it lit with natural light, the viewer can still reconstruct the natural image. Picasso, along with Braque, was an initiator and leading exponent of Cubism, a highly analytical theory of art that sought by means of a narrow range of colors and subject matter and by an exclusion of representational light, atmosphere, and conventional perspective to depict objects as they are known, not as they appear. Cubists moved more and more toward abstraction until the only reality left to them was the picture itself. Viewers who habitually regarded the spatial illusions of the fixed picture plane were forced to rethink.

In 1911, Braque introduced words and numbers in a painting called *The Portuguese* (see Figure 29.2). The letters and numbers rested on a picture plane but not within a space receding from it.

The next step was to move to a space in front of the picture plane, and that phenomenon we call collage. The experience of collage prompted again the ancient Socratic question "What is real?" If an image of a real chair is drawn on a sheet of paper or painted on a canvas, or if part of the arm of a chair is sawed off and attached to a surface, which illusion conveys more reality? The notion of a "real image" raised a paradox in that, strictly speaking, illusion and reality do not co-exist. Such contradictions, however, were part of the cubist effort to develop new visual sensibilities.

Looking at Picasso's *Still Life with Chair Caning* (see Figure 29.3), we see alien materials—a coiled rope and simulated chair caning on oil cloth—pasted to an oval shape, not the Renaissance rectangle, and then painted upon. Scraps of the real world now *represent* part of an image within a composition, and they *present* their own identity. The scraps are metamorphosed with the subject matter of the collage into a new perceptual construct.

This brief overview on collage has two objectives: (1) to show that considerable options exist in the use of visual space, most of which are provoked through knowledgeable experimentation; and (2) to press you to perceive and question the operative concerns behind your

FIGURE 29.2. Georges Braque (1882–1963, French): *The Portuguese* (1911). Oil on canvas, 46⅛" × 32". Offentliche Kunstsammlung, Basel.

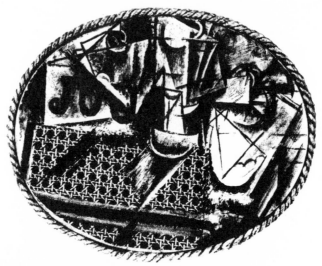

FIGURE 29.3. Pablo Picasso (1881–1973, Spanish): *Still Life with Chair Caning* (1911–1912). Paint and pasted oil cloth simulating chair caning, 10½″ × 13¾″, oval. Collection, the artist.

own act of drawing. Keep an open mind about the "framing" phenomenon characteristic of precut sheets of drawing paper.

But collage in the cubist sense is a tangle of complexities for beginners who have hardly tested the principles of the Renaissance picture plane. The drawing exercise in this chapter is actually a mixed-media problem, not collage. It is similar to collage in that pieces of paper are to be pasted to a surface. But the scraps, rather than "presenting their own identity," will be used to unify a conventional illusionistic space once again. The paper shapes could be used as a linear skeleton over which you draw the rest of the composition. Or you could use the paper pieces as geometric shapes, value shapes, or color shapes combined with drawing.

One of your media should be a newspaper or a brown paper bag. Working several media collectively is a challenging task because the effect of each medium is distinct. For instance, India ink is very black. Place black ink next to vine charcoal and the results are harshly dramatic, having an arbitrary contrast, generally dissonant.

Run through a few brief compositions of the still-life setup, testing your chosen materials. If the materials do not work together as well

FIGURE 29.4. A student composition using mixed media (brown paper bag, charcoal, and ink).

FIGURE 29.5. A student composition using mixed media (brown paper bag, newspaper, and charcoal).

FIGURE 29.6. A student composition using mixed media (brown paper bag, chalk, and ink).

FIGURE 29.7. A student composition using mixed media (brown paper bag, newspaper, graphite, and ink).

Collage and Mixed Media

as you anticipated, substitute something else until you strike a combination that does not violate the sense of receding space.

Tearing pieces of the newspaper or brown paper bag seems more appealing than cutting because of the element of chance involved in the tearing. Tearing utilizes less control than cutting, and more often than not the torn edge and shape are more interesting for that reason than the mechanical, impersonal edges produced by scissor cutting. You just might tear an idea into being.

Remember this maxim while using torn paper shapes: as in all drawing, it is necessary to move beyond duplicated object shapes such as bottles, vases, and people in order to establish substance in spatial relationships. Because you can hold in your hand a "piece of space" torn from brown paper, be careful that you do not resort to object duplication.

This problem lets you literally tear out, hold, place, and glue "pieces of space," and it could be confusing for you to incorporate drawing with pasted paper pieces. Nevertheless joining "pieces of space" with drawing is the crux of this problem. Try overlapping of shapes or try drawing from the torn shapes directly onto the drawing paper.

Measure your impulses against your judgment. Careful adjustments can make a great difference. Push and pull the weights, densities, shapes, lines, and values throughout the composition for the best composition (see Figures 29.4, 29.5, 29.6, and 29.7). Experience the shapes and space you are working with. In a word, move with your work until it moves you.

30

VARIATIONS

This chapter sets forth exercises which can extend experiences started elsewhere in the book. At this stage you must be somewhere between beginning and advanced drawing. You have most of the basic information that can be taught. Practice refines your learning experiences. Suggested below are variations on the basic problems you have already solved.

VARIATIONS

(1) An interesting approach to *perspective* lies in purposely drawing several horizon lines and vanishing points as part of the same drawing. In trying this, however, keep the illusion of space at least rationally distorted, not randomly distorted. Stay with the ground rules of basic perspective as you play with this problem. And remember, the composition needs to be devised before completing the drawing so that the differing perspectives will work to achieve a unity. Hogarth's work is a satire on perspective mistakes (see Figure 30.1) while Dali uniquely unifies his subject by placing us above and below Christ simultaneously (see Figure 30.2).

(2) A more precise approach for achieving *linear perspective* derives from early principles outlined separately by Brunelleschi and Alberti, but combined into a procedure called the "common" or "office"

FIGURE 30.1. W. Woolett after William Hogarth (1697–1764, English): *Satire on False Perspective*, frontispiece to Kirby's *Perspective of Architecture* (1761). Engraving. Museum of Fine Arts, Boston.

FIGURE 30.2. Salvador Dali (b. 1904, Spanish): *Crucifixion* (1951). Oil on canvas, 80⅝″ × 40⅝″. Glasgow Art Gallery and Museum.

method. This method will be applied to two-point perspective first because this use occurs most often in drawing and because the general principles for it are also characteristic of one- and three-point perspective.

Two-Point Perspective: Common Method

One building is seen from two positions: one is an overhead (floor) *plan* view, like a blueprint, identifying lengths and widths. The other is the same building, seen in *perspective* view, identifying height, width, and depth, as though you were standing some feet away, looking at the corner and two sides of the building.

The plan view containing the length and width of the building will be the basis from which you draw lines that extend directly into the perspective drawing, creating illusory depth (see Figure 30.3).

For practice, duplicate, step by step, the illustration using graph paper, a ruler, a protractor, and a very sharp pencil.

For the Overhead Plan View

Draw the top edge of the picture plane (PP), seen as a line.

Position the building above the line. One corner touches the picture plane. (Artists rarely place building corners on the picture plane, whereas architects often do to describe a scale for height.)

Position the station point (SP) below the picture plane. The station point is where you are standing. Remember, the station point has to account for two factors.

1. your *lateral* relationship (right, middle, left) to the building.

2. your *distance from* the building, dictated by the cone of vision and by the picture plane that encompasses the height and width of the building.

First place the lateral position of the station point.

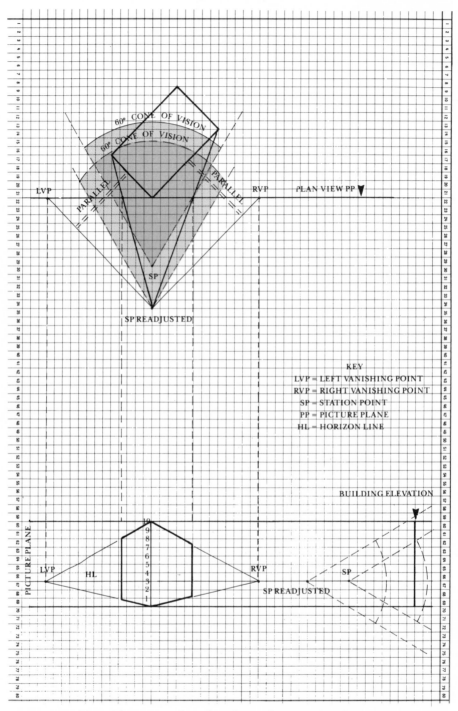

FIGURE 30.3. Two-point perspective, plan view and perspective view.

Variations

From that point, draw a line (the central sight line) vertical to the picture plane line and through the building. This will become the center of your drawing, though not necessarily the center of interest.

———————

To find the distance from the building, extend the central sight line below the picture plane line to a point where the angle of the cone of vision encompasses the width of the building. To place that angle, use a protractor. A 30-degree to 60-degree cone is common. That distance should coincide with your lateral position. The two together will give you the station point. (A few steps later, the station point and cone of vision will be checked in relation to the height of the building.)

———————

To identify the vanishing points on the picture plane, position a right angle at the station point so that lines drawn from the station point will remain parallel to the sides of the building. Those lines establish the right vanishing point (RVP) and left vanishing point (LVP) when they intersect the picture plane.

———————

From each boundary point (corner) of the building, lightly draw a line to the station point. Those *points of intersection* on the picture plane become the points from which lines will be dropped into the perspective plan to define the corners of the building in perspective.

For the Perspective View

Drop below the station point a few squares and draw the top edge of the picture plane across the sheet. It doesn't matter how many squares you drop, but you must leave enough graph paper to draw the perspective view. (Since the closest corner of the building touches the picture plane, the picture plane has to be as tall as that corner in scale. Assume this building is ten squares high.)

———————

Draw the base line of the picture plane.

———————

Draw the horizon line, equivalent to the height of your eyes or, for our purposes, three squares from the base of the picture plane.

The station point in *plan* view may not be accurately placed when the vertical dimensions are seen. It may need adjustment closer to or farther from the building. Verify the station point to the height of the building with an "elevation" or side view of the building. To the far right on the perspective picture plane, a vertical line, the height of the picture plane, will simulate a wall of the building. From that wall, duplicate the distance of the station point equivalent to that previously established in *plan* view, staying on the horizon line. At that point, if the 30-degree to 60-degree vertical cone of vision does not encompass the height of the building wall, move the station point accordingly. Then reposition the station point in *plan* view and redraw the boundary point lines to the new station point.

Since one corner of the building is against the picture plane in *plan*, drop a line from that point of intersection straight down and through the *perspective* picture plane. That establishes the corner of the building and its height.

Drop the left vanishing point (LVP) and right vanishing point (RVP) to the horizon line.

Roof lines and foundation lines (receding parallel lines) need to be drawn to the left vanishing point and right vanishing point from the building corner.

Determining the left and right visible corners is the next step. From the respective points of intersection at the *plan* picture plane, drop lines straight down to intersect the receding parallel lines of the building.

Erase the lines not needed, and the cubelike building is in perspective.

Variations

You might want to experiment by drawing windows and doors on the practice building. That exercise will help you in another problem, which describes the exact placement of walls and furniture in a room.

One-Point Perspective: Common Method

In one-point perspective, receding parallel lines converge to one point in the middle of your cone of vision. The room and its contents must be parallel to the picture plane.

Again, there will be two views. One room is seen from two positions: an overhead (floor) plan view, like a blueprint, identifying lengths and widths; and the same room, seen in *perspective* view, identifying height, width, and depth as though you were standing some feet away looking through one of the walls, which, in this case, becomes the picture plane.

The *plan* view, containing the length and width of the room and its contents, will be the basis from which you draw lines that extend directly into the *perspective* drawing, creating illusory depth.

This one-point perspective problem is broken down into two sequences, each using *plan* and *perspective* views. The first sequence describes placing walls and equal units in depth (see Figure 30.4). The second describes heights in depth and placement of furniture (see Figure 30.5). For practice, duplicate step by step the illustration, using graph paper, a ruler, a protractor, and a very sharp pencil.

For the Overhead Plan View (A)

The scale is 1 foot to two squares on the graph paper.

In the middle of the graph paper at the top, draw a room 12′ wide × 15′ long (24 × 30 squares). The 12-foot line closest to you is the plan-view picture plane seen on its top edge.

Place the station point (SP) below the picture plane (PP), 6 feet from

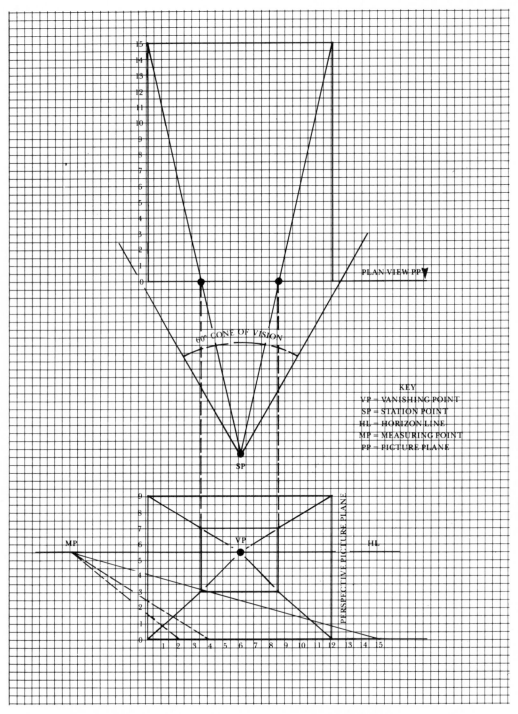

FIGURE 30.4. One-point perspective, plan view and perspective view A.

Variations

the side walls (midpoint) and far enough away so that the 30-degree to 60-degree cone of vision encompasses the width of the room.

From the station point, draw the central sight line through the room.

Lightly draw a line from each corner of the back wall to the station point.

For the Perspective View (A)

Below the station point a few squares and *directly below* the walls of the floor *plan,* drop lines to coincide with the *perspective* room walls when you begin to draw a rectangle 9 feet high × 12 feet wide (18 × 24 squares). Completing the rectangle forms the *perspective* picture plane. (Since the station point already encompasses the 12-foot width, it will also contain the 9-foot height and there is no problem with its placement.)

On the left vertical side of the picture plane, number 0 through 9. Along the base line (ground line) number 0 through 12. Numbers along the bottom and one side of the picture plane identify scale at the picture plane. From those numbered heights, receding parallels are drawn establishing a specific height in depth.

Draw the horizon line (HL) at $5\frac{1}{2}$ feet, passing through both walls.

Drop a line from the station point to intersect the horizon line. That point becomes the vanishing point (VP).

The side walls of the room are next. They begin at the corners of the picture plane and recede to the vanishing point. When the vertical corner lines of the back wall are dropped and intersect the receding lines, the side walls are identified.

From each corner of the picture plane, draw a line to the vanishing point.

────────────

And from the *plan* view picture plane, drop the back-wall corner lines to intersect the receding parallel lines of the side walls you just drew. The side walls are identified.

────────────

Complete the back wall with two horizontal lines, one between the ceiling intersection points and one between the floor intersection points. Erase the lines you do not need. The back wall is exactly 15 feet away from the picture plane.

────────────

The last thing to establish before placing the door, window, and table is the measuring point (MP), a pivot point on the horizon line used to measure receding 1-foot units. To locate the measuring point, the number that corresponds to the depth of the room has to be used— in this case, 15 feet.

────────────

Extend the base line of the picture plane from number 12 to number 15. Then from number 15 place the ruler diagonally so that it *passes through the bottom left corner of the back wall and proceeds to the horizon line*. (This procedure can be done on either side of the wall.) That point where the line converegs with the horizon line becomes the measuring point. Mark that point.

From the measuring point, with the ruler aligned to each number on the base line, 1 through 15, mark only the intersection points on the bottom left floor-wall line. This step identifies 1-foot units in depth.

────────────

Having now established the fifteen 1-foot units in receding space, you have the basic information necessary to complete the room with its furniture.

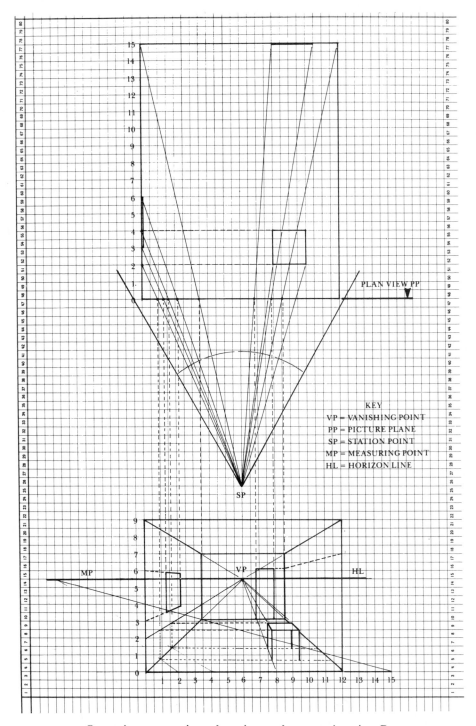

KEY

VP = VANISHING POINT
PP = PICTURE PLANE
SP = STATION POINT
MP = MEASURING POINT
HL = HORIZON LINE

FIGURE 30.5. One-point perspective, plan view and perspective view B.

Plan View (B)

Complete the overhead drawing, including the door, window, and table. (Note the lengths and widths from the scale drawing. Dimensions will be given when necessary.)

––––––––––

From each boundary point of each item drawn, lightly draw a line to the station point.

Perspective View (B)

The door on the Back Wall. The door is 7 feet high. Begin with the vertical 7-foot mark on the picture plane. From that mark, a line drawn to the vanishing point will intersect the back left wall corner at 7 feet. (Seven feet at the back wall appears shorter than at the picture plane.) From that intersection point, a horizontal line across the back wall gives you the door's height.

––––––––––

From the *plan* view picture plane, drop the corresponding lines (of the door's boundaries) into the *perspective* room to the floor, intersecting the horizontal just drawn, completing the door. Erase the lines you do not need.

––––––––––

The Window on the Left Wall. The window is 3 feet in from the picture plane, 3 feet up from the floor, and measures 3′ × 3′. From the vertical 3-foot and 6-foot mark on the picture plane, draw receding parallel lines to the vanishing point, identifying the top and bottom lines of the window.

––––––––––

From the *plan* view picture plane, drop the window's corresponding vertical boundaries to intersect the receding parallels just drawn, completing the window on the wall.

––––––––––

Erase the lines you do not need.

––––––––––

The Table in the Room. Exact heights in space begin at the vertical picture plane, then move in and away from the viewer. Separate components of the table unit are found, step by step, before the table can be completed. In this example, each step is begun at the picture plane, moved in along the wall, and then taken into the room with horizontal lines. Verticals are dropped from the *plan*-view picture plane to complete the object.

The Leg Placement on the Floor, Front and Back. The table is 2-feet in from the picture plane, 2 feet from the right wall, and measures $2' \times 2' \times 2'$. Count in 2 feet on the left floor measurement marks and draw a horizontal line across the room. The front table legs will rest on that line.

Count in 4 feet on the left floor measurement marks (the table is 2 feet long), and draw a horizontal line across the room. The back table legs will rest on that line.

From the *plan* picture plane, drop the corresponding vertical boundary lines of the table, front and back, to the horizontal lines. The four legs are positioned.

The Table Top, Front and Back. From the 2-foot vertical marking on the picture plane (the table is 2 feet high), draw the receding height line along the wall to the vanishing point. Since the table is 2 feet away from the picture plane, count in 2 feet again on the floor. Place your pencil there, then move vertically up to intersect the receding line you just drew. That gives you the height of the table at the wall.

Now, from that intersection point on the wall, move a horizontal line across to intersect the front legs, making the front table-top edge.

Do the same for the back table-top edge, beginning at the 4-foot floor mark. (the table is 2 feet long.)

Complete the table by connecting the front corners to the back corners with receding parallel lines, which should, if continued, converge at the vanishing point.

———————

Erase the lines you do not need.

———————

There are several short cuts one can use in placing objects, but this more detailed method provides a dependable registration for checking accuracy.

EXERCISES

1. Use some imagination and place more furniture and windows in the room. Find a room of special interest. Duplicate actual heights, widths, and depths. Use the common method, drawing both views on the graph paper. Then try drawing the same room freehand.

2. Practice drawing a set of stairs with the common method, both views. Then draw the stairs freehand.

3. Practice drawing an enlarged block letter of the alphabet such as a *T, H,* or an *L* (in perspective). Try the common method first. Then try drawing the same letter freehand.

Three-Point Perspective: Common Method

Three-point perspective will be described very briefly and illustrated. To draw a three-point perspective, you look up or down, tilting the cone of vision and thus the picture plane. The station point needs to be far enough away so that the width of the object (building, mountain, tree, statue) is not distorted.

Once the station point and central sight line have been determined, the picture plane is drawn perpendicular to the central line of sight, as illustrated (see Figure 30.6), and appears slanted.

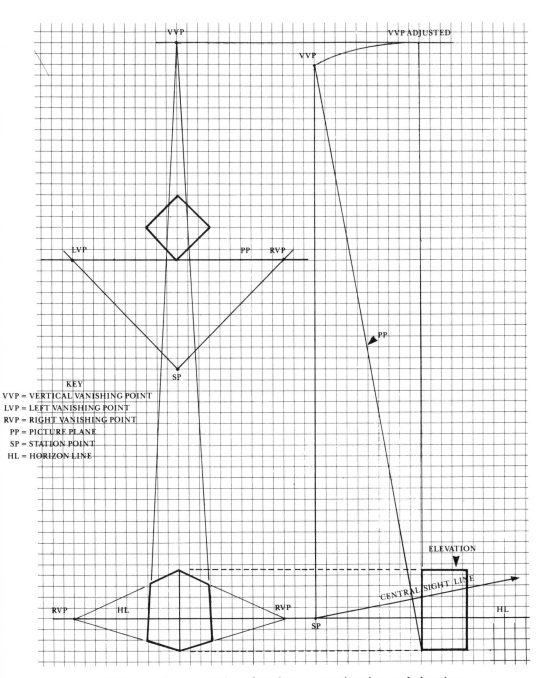

FIGURE 30.6. Three-point perspective, plan view, perspective view, and elevation.

In the elevation plan, the vertical vanishing point is located on (or beyond) the picture plane when a vertical line extending up (just point) from the station point intersects with the picture plane.

Since the picture plane is inclined at an angle to the ground, it must be pivoted vertically to the ground before the actual perspective drawing can be completed.

OTHER VARIATIONS

(3) While practicing with *cross contour,* your scanning can be horizontal, vertical, and diagonal in the same drawing, according to the curvilinear shapes of your setup. But keep those shapes as your main concern, not simply filling in objects with lines (see Figure 30.7).

(4) *Gesture* drawing can have variation on variation. A good practice session in gesture involves the use of memory. Look at a model for twenty seconds, memorizing the pose. Then close your eyes and draw a twenty-second gesture of the pose, putting as much emphasis as possible on areas of stress in the body. Be sure the model holds the pose as you

FIGURE 30.7. Student drawing in cross contour.

draw so that when you open your eyes you can check your drawing, and memory, against the original.

Always keep in mind the whole space you will be using as you draw. Even with closed eyes, you should be able to sense the whole sheet of paper on which a figure is to be placed. This is a strenuous exercise, but very helpful.

(5) Another approach to *gestures* is drawing them while in a very dark room, viewing a model that is spotlighted, with the spotlight the only light in the room. The gestures should be sixty seconds, with 5-minute breaks every twenty-five minutes for the model, for two hours. This approach is a strong, rich learning experience in that you must concentrate on translating what you see by not looking at the paper. Looking too much at the paper in the early stages of drawing keeps you concerned about the effect of the drawing and allows you to draw from an inaccurate and unrefined memory.

(6) Try *gesture* drawing of a figure for one hour, sixty-second poses (that means sixty drawings), with your pencil in the other hand. Right-handed drawers should draw with the left hand, and vice versa. The purpose here is to involve and challenge the undeveloped side of your brain and physical self to a participation in visual thinking. Indeed, just as sculpting offers a two-handed process, so is the thinking required for gesture drawing.

(7) A *three-tone* problem can work with any three adjacent values on a value scale, whether you use only three light values, three dark values, or three middle values. A variation like this gives you practice in very close value harmonies by using three values at the top of the value scale or three values at the middle value scale or three values at the bottom value scale.

(8) The *three-tone* drawing can be expanded another way for those who are particularly caught up with this problem. Five tones, seven tones, ten tones, almost any number will work. Overlapping one value of ink on another gives an intermediate value, increases the complexity of the drawing, and usually makes the work more interesting. There comes a point, however, where too many overlaid values become muddy. Avoid mud.

FIGURE 30.8. Student composition using an eraser as the drawing tool.

(9) Working in *values* with charcoal while using an eraser as one of the drawing tools builds information as you alternate charcoal strokes with eraser strokes. Cover the whole sheet of light colored charcoal paper with vine charcoal. Blow off the residue. That is your middle value. Lay in the compositional perimeters and establishing lines. Then, by erasing with a kneaded eraser, pull off the middle tones and work toward the lightest value shapes. Move into the darkest value shapes with more vine charcoal. Alternate the strokes of vine charcoal and eraser as you build the forms in your drawing (see Figure 30.8).

(10) A less-is-more problem in *values* and *contour* means drawing with the fewest lines and values possible to suggest forms in a composition. What minimum number of strokes identify a figure, landscape, or still life? Say the most with the least (see Figures 30.9, 30.10, 30.11, and 30.12).

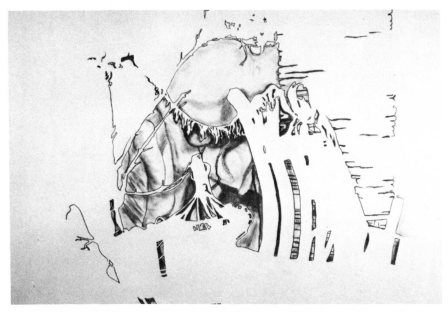

FIGURE 30.9. Student drawing using the fewest lines and shapes to identify subject matter (chair, reeds, birdcage, drapery, and bamboo screen).

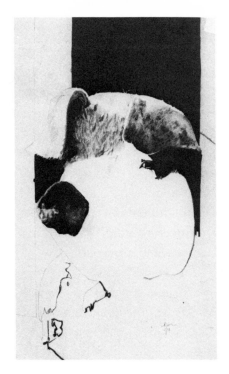

FIGURE 30.10. Student drawing using the fewest lines and shapes to identify subject matter (a pig's head).

FIGURE 30.11. Student drawing using the fewest lines and shapes to identify subject matter (female nude, seen from behind, seated on material).

FIGURE 30.12. Student drawing using the fewest lines and shapes
to identify subject matter (girl leaning against a chair).

Part Eight

MATTING

31

MATTING: SIMPLE
AND STANDARD

TOOLS
5 mat boards (30" × 40")
1 or 2 sheets of oaktag
pencil
mat knife
ruler
T-square and/or triangle
metal yardstick
clear acetate
cloth tape or brown gummed tape
masking tape (only for use on the acetate)
transparent plastic tape

Emphasis must be placed on the fact that both approaches to matting outlined here, which I call the "simple" and the "standard," are temporary (six months to one year) framing methods used to produce protective coverings until the drawing can be encased in a professional frame with mat, glass, a barrier paper to prevent yellowing, a styrofoam backing board, hooks, and hanging wire.

Encased in a wood, metal, fiberglass, or heavy plastic frame, a drawing or painting properly matted under glass is more permanently protected than encasing a piece of work inside a mat wrapped in acetate.

Professional framing accommodates several things: the contraction and expansion of various weights (thicknesses) of papers used; the prevention of damage to the drawing or painting from the weight of the glass; and the retardation of yellowing.

If the mat board is made of wood pulp, the professional framer should line the window mat piece with a 100-percent rag paper, called a barrier paper, or use a clear polyester sheet (.002 or .003 millimeters thick) similar to acetate. He should also place a barrier paper between the drawing or painting and the backing board.

To prevent discoloration, shrinkage, or swelling caused by humidity and heat, drawings or paintings on 100-percent rag paper, with 100-percent rag mats and backing boards, can be hermetically sealed, all air withdrawn from inside the frame. This vacuum method is the only safe long-range method, but expensive. It is used mainly by museum personnel who handle valuable works of art in heavily polluted areas. For our purposes, however, the simple and the standard processes will be employed. Many kinds of mat boards are available. Mat boards usually have two colors, one on either side, such as white/off-white, or white/gray. Some mat boards are cloth-backed, textured with a linen-like surface, or pebbled. Some are relatively thick, some thin.

A good rule to follow for beginning matting is to buy white/off-white 1/16-inch mat boards, pebbled or plain, because they are the cheapest, the most versatile, and the most easily cut. The cloth-backed boards cause trouble for novices since the cloth does not cut well with a mat knife. The thicker mat boards are too thick to cut well without a professional's mat cutter.

The mat knife should not have a spring-operated retractable blade. For the amount of pull and pressure put on the blade, buy a mat knife whose handle needs unscrewing in order to move the grooved blade forward and backward. The screw-handle type is safer.

T-squares are handy, of course, but expensive. If you can borrow a metal T-square, use that. T-squares with plastic edges get damaged easily from miscalculated cutting. A metal yardstick works as an alternative, but it needs to be held immobile while cutting along its edge.

Clear acetate comes in several thicknesses, called weights. Test several weights to see what works best. The lighter weights tend to be more workable while the heavier acetate cracks and tears readily. Plastics are inert, so acetate and styrofoam backing boards can be used without fear of discoloring papers or mats.

When taping any part of the drawing to any part of any mat board, *use a cloth tape* because it has a nonacidic backing (mulberry glue or a rice-starch glue) that sticks when wet and will not damage the drawing. Most art stores carry this kind of tape.

If the cloth tape is unavailable, the next best type is a good quality brown paper tape which will stick when wet. Caution must be used with paper tape, however. Often, too much water is used, and the drawings become wrinkled.

Masking tape is never used on drawings for two reasons:

    1. the acid in the gummed backing ruins the drawings;

    2. after a short time, changes in heat and humidity cause the tape to come off.

However, masking tape can be used on acetate.

SIMPLE MATTING

Simple matting is the process of measuring, cutting, and then placing a mat-board frame around a drawing. There are a number of ways to mat. The description of the methods that follow can be used as guides.

Cut four strips of paper lengthwise from one sheet of 18″ × 24″ newsprint, about 4½ inches wide. The strips should be adjusted individually on top of the drawing fo find the best framing space for the image. Keep in mind "breathing room." If the drawing is a figure, seated, facing left, you might need to move the left strip farther left to accommodate the space the sight line infers. When placed too close to the figure, a frame can squeeze the space and make it look chunky and chopped off. No hard and fast rules exist for the best framing of a composition. Use your judgment in selecting the framing space.

When you have decided on the framing space of the drawing, use your right-angle device, T-square, or triangle to achieve 90-degree corner angles. Then place one very small light pencil dot on the drawing in each corner where the paper strips converge to form an angle (see Figure 31.1).

FIGURE 31.1. Steps in matting: plastic right angle, pencil, dot.

Remove the strips of newsprint.

If the image on the paper was drawn too high or too low, tilted, or more to one side than the other on the sheet of drawing paper, the framing space should be placed so that the drawing appears straightened.

The aligned dots have established the *inner framing edge,* height and width, which is the *interior measurement* of the mat board you will cut for a frame. The *outer framing edge* is the *exterior measurement* of the frame, height and width.

Matting: Simple and Standard

The width of the framing border, the distance between the inner and outer framing edges, depends on the size of drawing that is to be matted. Two broad basic proportional standards can be used:

1. use the same proportions for each of the four sides of the frame —a 3:3:3:3 ratio (not necessarily inches);

2. use the same proportions for three sides of the frame, but make the base wider—3:3:3:4 ratio (not necessarily inches).

Two-inch mat-board frames are usually too narrow on large drawings.

Decide on the ratio to be used and work that out in inches (for example, a 3:3:3:3 ratio could be 2½–2½–2½–2½ inches, or it could be 3–3–3–3 inches).

For our purposes here, 3 inches on all four sides will be used.

Measure the vertical distance between the dots. Then add vertical height plus 6 inches. Measure the distance between the dots horizontally. Then add horizontal width plus 6 inches. (If the ratio in inches had been 3:3:3:4, you could add vertical height plus 7 inches.) The total length in inches and the total width in inches gives you the exterior length and width measurements of the framing mat border.

Using the color side of the mat board that is closest to the color of the drawing paper, measure, and mark the exterior measurements for the border frame with pencil points or lines.

To prevent cutting damage on a table or floor, cover the surface with old newspapers. If the table has an accurate 90-degree top corner, place the large sheet of mat board at the table-corner edges, drop the T-square lip edge over the table edge, line up the exterior measurement marks, and then, using the mat knife, cut the piece of mat board front through back, pressing hard on the knife but pulling carefully.

With the other hand, stabilize the T-square and mat board with pressure, but *always keep your free hand behind the blade.*

If using the floor, with a metal yardstick, line up the yardstick with the pencil marks while using your knee and free hand to apply pressure on top of the yardstick over the mat board. Draw the mat knife steadily down the yardstick edge, keeping the pressure hand *behind the blade.*

Once the exterior frame edge is cut, measure in from the edges 3 inches, making two marks on each of the four sides of the mat framing piece. Be sure to double check for correct measurements. T-square the corner angles, and mark them lightly with a pencil (⌐) so that you will not cut beyond the corner angles (see Figure 31.2).

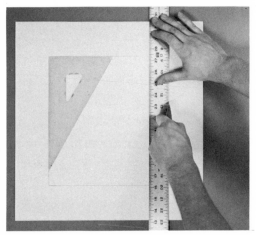

FIGURE 31.2. Steps in matting: free hand behind blade.

Begin cutting the same way for the interior measurements as you did the exterior measurement, lining up the marks with the T-square or the metal yardstick and cutting through the mat board, always keeping your pressure hand behind the cutting blade. (If a 3:3:3:4 ratio is used, the wide width is the base. Double check. Mistakes are often made here.)

Having completed both the exterior and interior cutting, you should have a 3-inch mat frame border.

***

Before taping the drawing to the border frame, be sure that your signature can be seen above the bottom inner frame edge.

The next sequence of steps describes a simple way of keeping the drawing aligned to the inner framing edges until you can turn the drawing and frame over to tape permanently.

Put a piece of sticky, removable tape on the top back and bottom back of the drawing, leaving half the length of the tape exposed beyond the drawing. Put the frame over the front of the drawing, matching the corners of the frame with the small corner dots on the drawing. Then, press the frame at the places where the sticky tape is. Turn the unit over. Now, on the back of the drawing, put one 2-inch strip of cloth tape at each of the top two corners and one in the middle at the top after removing the sticky tape (top and bottom). The drawing should now hang free from the top of the mat. Do not use any more tape on the drawing.

***

Cut a piece of oaktag to within $\frac{1}{2}$ inch of the exterior mat size. Place that over the drawing taped on the mat on the back, and tape the oaktag all the way around with the cloth tape or brown paper tape. Take care not to get the tape too wet. It may wrinkle on drying. Masking tape could be used to seal the oaktag too (see Figure 31.3).

The above is the most simple of the simple matting procedures. Another method of simple matting is done as follows.

***

Cut a piece of clear acetate 1 inch wider than the window all around. Tape the clear acetate over the window on the back of the frame, sealing it at the top with a transparent plastic tape. Center and tape the drawing on the frame as described before. Then, put a piece of oaktag as a safety sheet over the back of the drawing, sealing it to the back of the frame edge all the way around with tape (see Figure

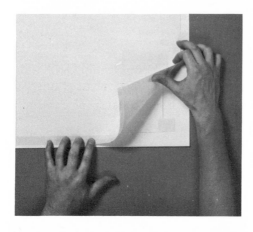

FIGURE 31.3. Steps in matting: tape drawing, oaktag.

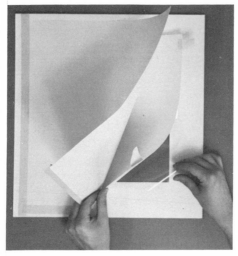

FIGURE 31.4. Steps in matting: frame, acetate, drawing, oaktag.

31.4). The oaktag should measure ½ inch less than the exterior measurement of the frame. (This method protects the front and back of the drawing.)

STANDARD MATTING

Standard matting is defined as matting a drawing with a mat frame border plus a backing board, sandwiching and wrapping the whole unit with acetate, and taping the acetate to the backing board.

Another method of standard matting is to cover just the window with acetate on the front mat instead of wrapping the whole unit with acetate. The "window" approach needs to be hinged, and accuracy is more difficult.

Matting: Simple and Standard

The first standard matting procedure should be experienced by everyone so that when drawings are carried, shipped, or used in shows, the appearance of the work is not diminished because of damage to exposed mats.

Follow the earlier directions for measuring, marking, and cutting a mat frame border.

———————

Cut a backing board of corrugated cardboard of mat board (preferably) the exact size of the exterior measurements of the front mat border. Remember, cardboard carries a high acidic content—you may want to line the backing board with a piece of plastic or rag paper.

———————

Center the drawing on the backing board so that when the front mat frame is temporarily placed over it, the drawing with dotted corners matches the top frame window corners. See that your signature shows.

———————

After the alignment has been made, remove the front mat frame, holding the drawing in place on the backing board.

———————

Because the tape should never touch the front of a drawing, mark with a pencil a point at the top two corners of the drawing paper on the backing board for positioning the drawing.

———————

Cut four strips of cloth tape approximately 1½″ × ½″. Place one strip vertically near each top corner of the drawing on the back, letting the strip extend beyond the drawing paper. Moisten the tape and press the strips to stick.

———————

Turn the drawing face up and align the corners of the drawing with the pencil-dot marking on the backing board. Moistening the last two strips one at a time, place each strip horizontally over the tape extensions of the drawing, and press each to the backing board. The tape now holds the drawing in place on the backing board, the tape resembling a cross.

———————

That's all the taping on the drawing. The drawing hangs loose now from those strips at the top (see Figure 31.5).

Now, place the front frame over the drawing.

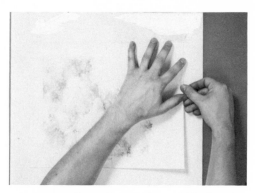

FIGURE 31.5. Steps in matting: 1½-inch strips of cloth tape, drawing, backing board.

Measure and cut a piece of acetate that is 3 inches wider on all sides than the exterior measurement of the mat.

———————

Place the matted unit equidistant from the sides of the acetate.

———————

Miter the corners of the acetate by placing a ruler's edge at each corner tip of the mat, diagonally across the corner of the acetate. Mark that diagonal with a line. The distance from the corners of the acetate to that line has to be equal on both sides. Cut off the corner of the acetate. That will give you a mitered corner when the acetate is folded to the back of the mat (see Figure 31.6).

———————

Miter all four corners.

———————

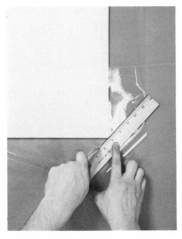

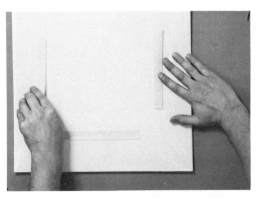

FIGURE 31.6. Steps in matting: ruler, acetate, miter.

FIGURE 31.7. Steps in matting: taped acetate pulled to back.

Heavy masking tape can be used in this next sequence. Cut strips several inches long, sticking each strip parallel to the acetate edge on which it is placed, leaving one half the width of the tape extended beyond the acetate and exposed so that the tape can stick to the backing board when the acetate is folded.

Pull the top and bottom acetate flaps simultaneously to the back, double checking to see that you have the corners properly aligned (see Figure 31.7).

Stick the tape to the backing board.

Put masking tape strips, as before, on the side flaps, and fold the side acetate flaps simultaneously to the back, sticking the tape to the backing board.

Reinforce the mitered corners of the acetate on the back of the mat board with tape, and run a second strip of tape all around the edges of the acetate on the back.

What you have now is a standard mat.

One other method of standard matting follows.

Cut the front and back mat as described earlier.

Put the front mat on top of the back mat (making sure you remember which is the bottom if you used a 3:3:3:4 ratio).

Lift the front up, over, back, and flat to the table top. This step is done so that a hinge can be made. Keep the top of the front mat touching the top of the back mat (see Figure 31.8).

Put a 3-inch strip of cloth tape at the corners, holding the two mats together. Put another 3-inch strip of cloth tape over the piece of tape you already have taped down. That reinforces the hinge.

If the mat is large enough, you may have to hinge it in one or two more places toward the center.

Lift the front window mat up, over, and down onto the backing mat. Slide the drawing between the two, aligning dots on the drawing to

FIGURE 31.8. Steps in matting: hinge 3-inch tape at corners.

match corners of the window frame as well as aligning your signature for visibility. Hold the drawing there.

———————

Lift the window frame back letting it fall flat to the table top.

———————

Mark with a pencil the two top corner points of the drawing paper on the backing board for positioning the drawing. Remove the drawing, cut the four 1½″ × ½″ strips, and paste one strip vertically near each corner, at the top on the back, letting the strip extend beyond the drawing paper. Turn the drawing over, face up, align the drawing with the dots, and moisten and place the other two strips horizontally over the vertical extensions, pressing them to the backing board. The drawing, again, hangs loose.

———————

Cut the acetate 1 inch wider than the front mat window on all four sides.

———————

Place the acetate above the top of the drawing on the backing board. Using the transparent plastic tape, seal the acetate across the top only.

———————

Let the acetate fall loose.

———————

Bring the window frame over now and the matting is done.

A few final suggestions.

While matting, if you err in a 3:3:3:4 ratio by cutting the 4-inch ratio at the side of the mat instead of the bottom, simply cut off one inch at the exterior edge of the widest side, giving your framing mat and backing board a 3:3:3:3 ratio.

If you measure the inner framing edge inaccurately, longer or wider, try adjusting the framing piece over the drawing. If the compromised realigned space worked well, fine. More often than not the space looks awkward and you are out of luck. A new mat needs to be cut.

Drawing on torn or ripped paper causes dilemmas. Sometimes a student's best work is done on a torn piece of scrap paper, but matting patched works betrays an amateur attitude. File torn works and use them as growth indices against which you test your maturing work.

FIGURE 31.9. Rembrandt Harmensz. van Rijn (1606–1669, Dutch): *Self-Portrait* (1659). Canvas, 33¼″ × 26″. National Gallery of Art, Washington, D.C.

NOTES

CHAPTER TWO. BLIND CONTOUR AND BALANCE IN COMPOSITION

1. Pliny the Elder, *The Elder Pliny's Chapters on the History of Art,* trans. K. Jex-Blake (St. Clair Shores, Mich.: Scholarly Press, 1968), p. 113.

CHAPTER EIGHT. LINEAR PERSPECTIVE

1. Samuel Y. Edgerton, Jr., *The Renaissance Rediscovery of Linear Perspective* (New York: Basic Books, 1975), p. 145.
2. Antonio di Tuccio Manetti, *The Life of Brunelleschi,* trans. Catharine Enggass (University Park, Pa.: Pennsylvania State University Press, 1970), p. 45.

CHAPTER FIFTEEN. A PROBLEM IN SCULPTURE—HEADS

1. Susanne K. Langer, *Feeling and Form* (New York: Scribners, 1953), p. 90.

CHAPTER EIGHTEEN. VALUE STUDIES

1. One such value finder, called the Modular Color Value Finder, is distributed by Permanent Pigments, Incorporated, Cincinnati, Ohio 45212.

CHAPTER TWENTY-FIVE. RESPONSIVE ANALYSIS: A CRITICAL METHOD

1. Heinrich Wölfflin, *Principles of Art History* (New York: Dover, 1932), p. 124.
2. *Ibid.,* p. 5.
3. Richard Payne Knight and Thomas Wright, *Sexual Symbolism* (New York: Julian Press, 1957), p. 12.

CHAPTER TWENTY-SIX. EXPRESSION

1. Susanne K. Langer, *Feeling and Form* (New York: Scribners, 1953), p. 13.

BIBLIOGRAPHY

Arnason, H. H. *History of Modern Art.* New York: Prentice-Hall, 1969.

Ballinger, Louise Bowen. *Perspective/Space and Design.* New York: Van Nostrand Reinhold, 1969.

Berenson, Bernard. *The Florentine Painters of the Renaissance.* New York and London: Putnam, 1896.

Brockett, Oscar G. *The Theater, an Introduction.* New York and Chicago: Holt, Rinehart and Winston, 1964.

Canaday, John. *Keys to Art.* New York: Tudor, 1962.

D'Amelio, Joseph. *Perspective Drawing Handbook.* New York: Tudor, 1964.

Demargne, Pierre. *The Birth of Greek Art.* New York: Golden Press, 1964.

Edgerton, Samuel Y. *The Renaissance Rediscovery of Linear Perspective.* New York: Basic Books, 1975.

Elgar, Frank. *Cézanne.* New York: Abrams, 1969.

Goldstein, Nathan. *The Art of Responsive Drawing.* Englewood Cliffs, N.J.: Prentice-Hall, 1973.

Gombrich, E. H. *Art and Illusion.* Princeton: Princeton University Press, 1969.

Hafner, German. *Art of Crete, Mycenae, and Greece.* New York: Abrams, 1968.

Haftmann, Werner. *Painting in the Twentieth Century,* Vol. I. Washington: Praeger, 1965.

Hauser, Arnold. *The Philosophy of Art History.* New York: World, 1965.

Janson, H. W. *History of Art*. New York: Abrams, 1969.

Jones, W. T. *A History of Western Philosophy*. New York: Harcourt, Brace & World, 1952.

Kelly, Francis. *Art Restoration*. New York: McGraw-Hill, 1972.

Knight, Richard, and Thomas Wright. *Sexual Symbolism*. New York: Julian Press, 1957.

Kozloff, Max. *Cubism, Futurism*. New York: Charterhouse, 1972.

Langer, Susanne K. *Philosophy in a New Key*. New York: Mentor, 1953.

————. *Feeling and Form*. New York: Scribners, 1953.

Laning, Edward. *Perspective for Artists*. London: Pitman, 1967.

Lucie-Smith, Edward. *Thinking about Art*. London: Calder and Boyars, 1968.

Macgillavry, Caroline. *Symmetry Aspects of M. C. Escher's Periodic Drawings*. Utrecht: A. Oosthoek's Uitgeversmaatschappjj, 1965.

Manetti, Antonio di Tuccio. *The Life of Brunelleschi*, trans. Catherine Enggass. University Park, Pa.: Pennsylvania State University Press, 1970.

Mayer, Ralph W. *The Artist's Handbook of Materials and Techniques*, rev. ed. New York: Viking, 1970.

Mendelowitz, Daniel M. *Drawing*. New York: Holt, Rinehart and Winston, 1967.

Nicolaides, Kimon. *The Natural Way to Draw*. Boston: Houghton Mifflin, 1941.

Osborne, Harold, ed. *Oxford Companion to Art*. Oxford, Eng.: Clarendon Press, 1970.

Panofsky, Erwin. *The Life and Art of Albrecht Dürer*. Princeton, N.J.: Princeton University Press, 1955.

Patten, Lawton M., and Milton L. Rogness. *Architectural Drawing*. Dubuque, Iowa: Brown, 1962.

Peck, Stephen Rogers. *Atlas of Human Anatomy for the Artist*. New York: Oxford University Press, 1968.

Pliny the Elder. *The Elder Pliny's Chapters on the History of Art*, trans. K. Jex-Blake. St. Clair Shores, Mich.: Scholarly Press, 1968.

Poore, Henry Rankin. *Composition in Art*. New York: Sterling, 1967.

Bibliography

Purser, Stuart. *The Drawing Handbook*. Worcester, Mass.: Davis, 1976.

Rewald, John. *Paul Cézanne: A Biography*. New York: Shocken, 1968.

Rose, Bernice. *Drawing Now*. New York: The Museum of Modern Art, 1976.

Seiberling, Frank. *Looking into Art*. New York: Holt, Rinehart and Winston, 1959.

Watrous, James. *The Craft of Old-Master Drawings*. Madison, Wis.: University of Wisconsin Press, 1957.

Watson, Ernest W. *Perspective for Sketchers*. New York: Reinhold, 1964.

Wölfflin, Heinrich. *Principles of Art History*. New York: Dover, 1932.

Wolfram, Eddie. *History of Collage*. New York: Macmillan, 1975.

Wollheim, Richard, ed. *The Image in Form*. New York: Harper & Row, 1972.

INDEX

Abraham Caressing Isaac (Rembrandt), 209, 211

action gesture, 132–36
   motion, capturing, 132–33
   thinking "rhythmic figure," 136
   using a model, 133–36

Aeneid (Virgil), 62, 63

aerial perspective, 37–39, 79–80

affective statement, 246

Ambroise Vollard (Picasso), 96, 97, 263–64

analytical tracings, 225–31
   reducing shapes to geometric equivalents, 226
   selecting works for, 225–26
   sight line, 226–28
   test for accuracy, 231
   van der Weyden's *Descent from the Cross*, 228–31
   see also responsive analysis

anamorphosis, 68

animal studies in contour, 49–56
   density of line, 55
   finding an animal model, 49–50
   fur or feathers, 53–55
   kinds of lines, 50–51
   laying out the composition, 51–53

Annunciation (Martini), 76, 77

armature, 156–57

assorted supplies, 14, 15

Bacon, Francis, 241, 243–44

balance in composition, 36–43
   formal, 37

informal, division of thirds, 36–37
   perspective, 37–39
   symmetrical or asymmetrical, 41–43
   within (to the viewer), 39–41

blind contour, 27–43
   aim of, 31–32
   balance in composition, 36–43
   delineation, 27–28
   forefinger, 29–31
   model profile, 33
   shoe, 32
   spatial organization, 34–36
   through sense of touch, 34

body stress in gesture, 137–40
   adding overlay, 138–39
   getting the "feel," 137–38

Brangwyn, Sir Frank William, 148, 149

Braque, Georges, 264, 265

Bresdin, Rodolphe, 219, 220, 248, 249

brown-paper-bag medium, 266–69

Brueghel, Pieter, the Elder, 219

Brunelleschi, Filippo, 70–71, 270

brushes, 12–13

Byzantine Christ, 77

caoutchouc, 11

central sight line, 82

charcoal, chalk, and crayons, 9–11

chiaroscuro, 187

circles and centers in perspective, 94–96

Cold-Pressed papers (CP), 6

collage and mixed media, 263–69

compositions, gesture, 146–49

cone of vision, 82
contour line, 17–114
  animal studies in, 49–56
  blind, and balance in composition, 27–43
  cross, 59–64
  distortions, 65–69
  foreshortening in, 106–14
  image inversion, 57–58
  linear perspective, 70–105
  negative, 44–48
  three-tone pattern in, 165–72
conventional (or local) value, 193–95
copying temptation, 4
critical methodology, *see* responsive analysis
cross contour, 59–64
  lights and darks, 60–61
  position of approach, 60
  power of the sensitive line, 62–64
  use of space, 59, 61–62
  value in, 59, 60
  variations, 286
crosshatch, 209–14
  edges, 214
  values, building, 212–13
Crucifixion (Dali), 270, 272
cube, linear perspective and, 87–90

Dali, Salvador, 270, 272
da Vinci, Leonardo, 132, 133
Dead Christ, The (Mantegna), 112, 113
Descent from the Cross, The (van der Weyden), 228, 229
distortions, 65–69
  anamorphosis, 68
  by refraction, 65–68
Dog Scratching Itself (Housebook Master), 49, 50
drapery, value in, 196–205
  different materials, 198–99
  and problems in composition, 199–207
Drawing Hands (Escher), 186

elongated gesture, 160–64
equal units in depth, 93–94
erasers, 11–12
Escher, M. C., 186
Euclid, 73
experimentation, 253–90
  collage and mixed media, 263–69
  repeated images, 255–59
  selected composing, 260–62
  variations, 270–90

expression, 246–52
  form and idea, 246–50
  warnings, 250–51
expressive content, 246

Female Nude Seated and Bending Forward (Rembrandt), 238, 239–41
Flagg, James Montgomery, 108
Flight into Egypt, The (Bresdin), 248, 249
foreshortening in contour, 106–14
  difficulties with perspective, 112
  figure proportions, 108–12
  impact from, 108
  spatial relationships, 108
form and idea, 246–50
Francesca, Piero della, 108, 110
Frog and Flies (Ruscha and Price), 256

general gesture, 127–31
  confusion in (how to avoid), 131
  essential characteristics, 127–28
Gentile da Fabriano, Francesco di, 96, 97
gesture, 115–50
  action, 132–36
  body stress in, 137–40
  composition, 146–49
  elongated, 160–64
  general, 127–31
  reverse, 141–42
  variations, 286–87
  of walks, 143–46
Grand Arbre Noir, Le (Bresdin), 219, 220
graphite, 8–9
Greek vase painting, 165–66
grids, 53
ground, 192
Grove of Cypresses (Van Gogh), 63, 64

Haymaking (Brueghel the Elder), 219
Head Surrounded by Sides of Beef (Bacon), 241, 243–44
Hello (Lindner), 241–43
Hogarth, William, 209, 211, 270, 271
Holbein, Hans, the Younger, 68, 69
Holy Family Passing under an Arch, The (Tiepolo), 248, 249
Homer, Winslow, 98, 99
horizon line, 80–81
  using a cube (to help clarify), 87–90
  and vanishing points, 84–85
Hot-Pressed papers (HP), 6–7

Icy Fingers (Zimmerman), 219, 221

Index

illusory depth, how to achieve, 79–80
image inversion, 57–58
images, repetition of, 255–59
inclined planes, 87
ink and brushes, 12–13
integrative tension, 247
I Want You (Flagg), 108

Jean de Dinteville and Georges de Selves, or The Ambassadors (Holbein the Younger), 68, 69

Landscape (Thiebaud), 219, 220
landscape structure, two-day study, 215–21
  outdoor space and, 215–16
  repetitions of nature, what to do, 216–17
  scanning for a composition, 216
  values, working selectively, 217–19
Large Still Life with Coffee Pot (Morandi), 209, 210
Last Judgment, The (Ottonian), 71
La Tour, Georges de, 98
left vanishing point (LVP), 275, 276
light rays and cast shadows, 96–105
Lindner, Richard, 241–43
linear perspective, 70–105
  cube (to help clarify), 87–90
  exercises, 90–105
    circles and centers, 94–96
    equal units in depth, 93–94
    light rays and cast shadows, 96–105
    horizon line, 80–81
    illusory depth, 79–80
    vanishing point, 70, 83–87
    variations, 270–73
lined perspective, 37
Lord Lovat (Hogarth), 209, 211
Lying Man (Tintoretto), 108, 109

Magritte, René, 256, 257
Man's Head (Francesca), 108, 110
Mantegna, Andrea, 106, 107, 112, 113, 201, 202
Marie Sethe at the Piano (Rysselberghe), 213, 214
Martini, Simone, 76, 77
Masaccio, 77, 78
materials and shape (from which form will be realized), 247
mat knife, 294
matting, 291–306
  simple process, 295–300

standard, 300–6
tools needed, 293
media, 6–14
  assorted supplies, 14, 15
  charcoal, chalk, and crayons, 9–11
  erasers, 11–12
  ink and brushes, 12–13
  papers, 6–8
  pencils, 8–9
  testing, 14
Moore, Henry, 160, 161
Morandi, Giorgio, 209, 210
Morning Bell, The (Homer), 98, 99

Nativity (Gentile da Fabriano), 96, 97
negative contour, 44–48
  "either/or" areas, 46
  horizontal or vertical composition, 46–48
  reducing depth in, 46
  shapes of space, 44–46
newspaper media, 266–69

one-point perspective, 90, 277–84

papers, 6–8
  amount of, 7–8
Parmigianino, 65, 66
pencils, 8–9
  amount of, 9
pens, 13
perspective, 37–39
  aerial, 37–39, 79–80
  circles and centers in, 94–96
  defined, 79
  in foreshortening, 112
  linear, 70–105, 270–73
  of the original object, 73–75
  three-point, 89, 284–86
  two-point, 87, 273–77
  variations, 270–86
    approach to, 270
    linear, 270–73
    one-point, 277–84
    three-point, 284–86
    two-point, 273–77
Picasso, Pablo, 29, 96, 97, 263–64, 265, 266
picture plane, 82–83
point of view, 46
points of intersection, 275
Portuguese, The (Braque), 264, 265
Price, Kenneth, 256
Prud'hon, Pierre-Paul, 238–39

quill pens, 13

rag paper, 7
Rearing Horse, A (da Vinci), 132, 133
receding parallel lines, 84, 85
refraction, distortion by, 65–68
Rembrandt, 209, 211, 238, 239–41
Renée de Trois Quarts (Villon), 209, 210
repetition of images, 255–59
resolution, 247
responsive analysis, 232–45
  Bacon's *Head Surrounded by Sides of Beef*, 243–44
  Lindner's *Hello*, 241–43
  pitfalls to avoid, 245
  Prud'hon's *La Source*, 238–39
  Rembrandt's *Female Nude Seated and Bending Forward*, 239–41
  signals, 234–35
  tectonic and theatrical modes, 235–38
  tips for beginning critics, 233–34
  see also analytical tracings
reverse gesture, 141–42
reverse value studies, 192–95
  conventional (or local) value, 193–95
  "ground," 192
  meaning of, 193
right vanishing point (RVP), 275, 276
Rubens, Peter Paul, 108, 109
Ruscha, Ed, 256
Rysselberghe, Theo van, 213, 214

St. James Led to His Execution (Mantegna), 106, 107, 201, 202
St. Joseph the Carpenter (La Tour), 98
scale, 247
sculpture: heads, 153–59
  armature, 156–57
  eyes, 157
  hair, 159
  rotating the unit, 159
  scale drawing, 156
  shape of the head, 157
  space, 153
  what to do (before starting), 155–56
selected composing, 260–62
Self-Portrait (Parmigianino), 65, 66
shape and materials, 247
sight line, 226–28
Source, La (Picasso), 29
Source, La (Prud'hon), 238–39
Springtime (Brangwyn), 148, 149

squinting, 60–61
"stabilizing" the subject, 50–51
Stag Hunt (Gnosis), 55, 56
standard matting, 300–6
starting process, 3–6
  see also media
station point, 83
Still Life with Chair Caning (Picasso), 265, 266
Studies of Arms and Legs (Rubens), 108, 109
style and subject, 247
subject matter, 247
superficial technique, 4–6

tectonic and theatrical modes, 235–38
Thiebaud, Wayne, 219, 220
Thought Which Sees, The (Magritte), 256, 257
three-point perspective, 89
  variations, 284–86
three-tone drawing, 287
three-tone pattern in contour, 165–72
  finishing the work, 169–71
  in Greek vase painting, 165–66
  system to keep values identified, 169
  value shapes, 166–69
Tiepolo, Giovanni Domenico, 248, 249
Tintoretto, 108, 109
Trinity (Masaccio), 77, 78
T-squares, for matting, 294
two-point perspective, 87
  variations, 273–77
    for overhead plan view, 273–75
    for perspective view, 275–77

unstable compositions, 43

value, 173–221
  crosshatch, 209–14
  in drapery, 196–205
  landscape structure, two-day study, 215–21
  three lighting positions, 206–8
  transition into volume and pattern, 151–72
    elongated gesture, 160–64
    problem in sculpture: heads, 153–59
    three-tone pattern in contour, 165–72
  variations of working in, 288
value scales, 185–86

Index

value studies, 185–91
  color of paper, 189
  grouping each value, 188–89
  manipulating charcoal value shapes, 189–91
  meaning of, 187
  reverse, 192–95
  setting up, 188
van der Weyden, Rogier, 228, 229
Van Gogh, Vincent Willem, 63, 64
vanishing points, 70, 83–87
  finding, 85
  horizon line and, 84–85
  receding parallel lines, 84
  using a cube (to help clarify), 87–90
  vertical infinity line, 85–87
variations, 270–90
  cross contour, 286
  gestures, 286–87

  perspective, 270–86
  problem in values and contour, 288
  three-tone, 287
  working in values, 288
vertical infinity line, 85–87
Villon, Jacques, 209, 210
Virgil, 62, 63
volume, inferring, 165

walks, gestures of, 143–46
  differentiating choices, 146
  drawing "blind," 144
  incorporating clothing, 145
  varieties of walks, 144
  viewing a passer-by, 144
Women Winding Wool (Moore), 160, 161

Zimmerman, William, 219, 221

STUDENT CREDITS

Kathy Ambrose, Lee Britkrentz, Colleen Clark, Shirley Couture, John Coverdale, Denise Donaldson, Roger Erby, Nikki Finsand, Sue Fisher, Ann Gibbs, Pat Green, David Haberger, Heidi Hart, Lynn Heller, Pat Hertema, Terry Hilbert, Blaine Houmes, Dori James, Lee Ann Jefferson, Debra Jennings, David Jensen, Gaylen Johannsen, Janice Johnson, Robert Johnson, Kathy Kuster, Mark Mabry, Norman McInnes, Jon Martin, Berdina Mills, Wendy Mulligan, Margo Mumma, David Olson, Carol Passman, Anthony Pazos, Lisa Porter, Ann Howber Rowley, Carol Rueber, G. Ruiz, Teresa Russell, Donald Steffan, Joe Stein, Ed Stewart, Greg Thoennes, Robert Timberlake, Deb Underberg, Barbara Varnum, Cheri Watson, Doug Wilke, Nancy Williwams, Deb Wright.

PHOTO CREDITS

The Albright-Knox Art Gallery, Buffalo, New York: Figure 10.1.

Alinari: Figures 8.9, 8.11, 8.41, 9.2, 9.8, 20.6.

Alte Pinakothek, Munich: Figures 2.23, 2.31, 8.13f, Plate V.

Art Institute of Chicago: Figures 2.3, 2.4, 2.5, 6.6, 9.4, 10.6, 10.7, 10.8, 18.4, 18.5, 18.6,
      18.8, 18.10, 22.2, 22.5, 23.6, Plate X.

Baltimore Museum of Art: Figure 22.1.

Bayerische Staatsbibliothek, Munich: Figure 8.1.

British Museum, London: Figures 2.10, 8.13d, 9.1, 10.5, 18.1, 20.4, Plate VIII.

Brogi: Figure 8.31.

Sterling and Francine Clark Art Institute, Williamstown, Massachusetts: Plate VII.

The Cloisters Collection, Metropolitan Museum of Art, New York: Figure 20.5.

Des Moines Art Center: Figures 2.26, 6.5, 14.4, 15.1, 18.3, 18.7, 22.3, 22.4, 27.1.

George Fletcher: Figure 2.8.

Fogg Art Museum, Harvard University, Cambridge, Massachusetts: Figure 10.2.

Vladimir Fyman: Figure 23.4.

Gemeentemuseum, The Hague: Figures 18.12, 23.5.

Giraudon: Figures 2.7, 2.9, 2.28, 8.33, 17.2, 17.3, 20.1, 20.8.

Glasgow Art Gallery and Museum: Figure 30.2.

Hirmer: Figure 8.10.

Koninklijk Museum, Antwerp: Plate XII.

Kunsthalle, Hamburg: Figure 2.2.

Kunsthistorisches Museum, Vienna: Figures 7.1, 20.7.

Louvre, Paris: Figure 10.3, Plate VI.

Metropolitan Museum of Art, New York: Figures 2.30, 8.13g, 8.13i, 17.1, 18.9.

Musée de Picardie, Amiens: Figure 8.13h.

Museum Boymans–Van Beuningen, Rotterdam: Figure 9.5.

Museum Faesch, Basel: Figure 2.6.

Museum of Fine Arts, Boston: Figures 2.25, 30.1, Plate IV.
Museum of Modern Art, New York: Figures 2.11, 16.1, 27.2.
National Gallery, London: Figure 7.5.
National Gallery, Prague: Figure 23.4.
National Gallery of Art, Washington, D.C.: Figure 31.9.
Nelson Gallery—Atkins Museum of Fine Arts, Kansas City: Figure 2.29.
New York Public Library: Figures 8.4, 8.7, 8.8, 9.6, 26.1.
Offentliche Kunstsammlung, Basel: Figures 2.1, 29.2.
Pella Museum: Figure 4.8.
Prado, Madrid: Plate I.
Pushkin Museum, Moscow: Figure 8.32, 29.1.
Rheinisches Bildarchiv: Figure 10.4.
Rijksmuseum, Amsterdam: Figure 4.1.
Royal Library, Windsor Castle, London: frontispiece, Figure 11.1.
Sotheby Parke Bernet, London: Figure 18.2.
Staatliche Antikensammlungen, Munich: Figure 8.2.
Uffizi Gallery, Florence: Figure 20.6.
University Museum, Philadelphia: Figure 8.3.
Victoria and Albert Museum, London: Plate III.
Yale University Art Gallery, New Haven: Figures 8.13e, 8.34.